Conquer Your Kitchen...

M000110601

The Hungry Chick Dieting Solution Cookbook Reference Guide

Over 100 Surprising Kitchen Secrets That Will Not Only Help You To Eat Healthier But Still Provide Wholesome Meals That Your Entire Family Can Still Enjoy!

Chef Jai Scovers

J. Scovers Healthy Solutions

Disclaimer: Losing weight depends on your commitment to eating healthier and exercising. Your results will differ based on your weight loss efforts.

That's why you should ALWAYS consult YOUR primary care doctor before starting any weight loss, weight management, fitness or health related program, even if it's written or has been organized by a professional or expert in that field. No one but your primary care doctor knows your medical history.

Your health is your most important asset. Please don't risk it by ignoring or not seeking advice from your medical professional before starting anything that may put your health at risk. Results with any weight loss plan will vary. The information provided is a based on the author's beliefs and research.

The author and publisher specifically disclaims all responsibility for any liability, loss or risk, personal and otherwise, which is incurred as a direct or indirect consequence from the use or the application of any and/or all content from this book. This information is presented solely for its educational value only.

Conquer Your Kitchen... The Hungry Chick Dieting Solution Cookbook Reference Guide

Copyright © 2015 by J. Scovers and R.A. Clark

ISBN: 0-9799302-5-1 ISBN-13: 978-0-9799302-5-6

Published by J. Scovers Health Solutions, a division of March Third Imprints in the United States of America.

Dedication...

This book is dedicated to God, who is the one that make everything possible. Of whom God gives much, much is required. Because, who we are is a gift from God and who we become is our gift to God.

I dedicate this book to my mother, Elizabeth Louise Clark, who is my daily inspiration to be a better person and to always do what I can to help other people live better and become better people for themselves.

I also dedicate this book to strong women everywhere. I don't care if you are a size zero or a fourteen. I understand your struggle to love yourself in a world, where because of our size; we often forget to love ourselves.

I hope that you enjoy what I have shared...

Chef Jai

Table of Contents...

- You Have A Choice... 7
- Mise En Place... 11
- What Every Home Chef's Kitchen Needs... 16
- The Most Important Thing In Your Home... 19
- Meal Planning 101... 24
- Creating Your Plate... 28
- I Know That You Still Have Questions... 33
- Drinking Water 101... 39
- Eating The Right Amount Of Calories 101... 43
- How To Read Even Your Basic Food Labels... 46
- Calorie Counting 101... 48
- Basic Cooking Terms... 59
- Pantry Basics 101... 66
- Herbs & Spices 101... 69
- Simplified Measurements... 73
- Food Substitutions... 76
- Kitchen Safety 101... 79
- The Truth About Food Safety... 81
- Food Storage 101... 85
- How To Read Food Label Dates... 89
- Refrigerator And Freezer Storage Times... 91
- Egg Storage Chart... 94
- Food Thermometers... 96
- Safe Minimum Cooking Temperatures... 97

- Roasting 101... 99
- Slow Cooking 101... 101
- Storing And Keeping Fresh Vegetables... 108
- Veggie Cooking Times... 112
- Perfect Pasta 101... 114
- Pasta Cooking Times... 117
- Baking 101... 120
- Meal Quick Fixes... 126
- Simple, Healthy & Delicious Recipe Sampler...129
- Index... 133

You Have A Choice...

If you are like me, you love to eat, but hate to diet. You want or need to watch your weight, but hate to give up the joys of cooking or the pleasure that you find when you try different foods and drinks.

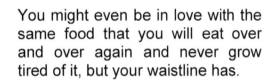

You might even be in love with the same food that you will eat over and over again and never grow tired of it, but your waistline has.

You might also be looking for ways to help yourself cut down on calories, cholesterol, preservatives, salt, and/or unhealthy fats without that awful feeling that you get from some so called "healthy foods" that still leave you feeling hungry. Trust me, I know the feeling.

Then, there are those among us who love to eat at home, but you have very little time to cook a complex meal, or even, a complete meal for that matter. What happens if you have a family? How do you lose weight when you still have to face the daily challenge of providing a wholesome meal for your spouse and/or your children?

Trust me, it is hard enough when the only person you have to answer to is yourself, but if you have a family, there are even more factors to consider when cooking any meal, such as their likes and dislikes, or even, food allergies.

One of the biggest obstacles that I have found that many people face on a diet is trying to maintain that diet, but being forced to sit through meals filled with foods that your diet said that you can't have. Or even being forced to stick to eating only certain foods. No grains? No meats? No dairy?

Then, there is the problem, when your life tends to move at such a fast pace, that it has redefined the way that you eat. With little time to cook, fast food, take out foods and eating out are not just unhealthy temptations anymore, they are the norms in our lives and for our families, when they don't have to be. Trust me, I know! I am a chef! My entire life is based on people not wanting to cook at home.

What happens when you do eat out? For a minute, I want you to stop pretending to be content with a side salad and a Diet Pepsi or Diet Coke, when your family or spouse is eating burgers and fries. Let me ask you again, whoever said that you should have to starve yourself to make this happen? Well, now with "Conquer Your Kitchen... The Hungry Chick Dieting Solution Cookbook Reference Guide," and the companion book, "Simple, Healthy & Delicious... The Hungry Chick Dieting Solution Cookbook" you don't have to.

Did you know that by cooking at home with some of the kitchen secrets and tips that you will find in this book, at least twice a week, will help you to reduce the amount of fats, cholesterol, preservatives and calories in the meals that you eat? Just two times per week can change your life.

You see, cooking at home doesn't have to be a problem, especially when you have children. Instead, let me show you how to use it as an opportunity to teach your children good eating habits that can last a lifetime. Making healthy decisions about your life and the lives of the people that you love actually start with a home cooked meal.

With each new meal that you bring to the table, you'll learn how to shift the focus away from your attempts to lose weight to knowing how much better that you will feel, knowing that your entire family is feeling better, looking better, eating better and having more energy.

"Conquer Your Kitchen" was designed to show you how to make wholesome meals that are healthy, quick and delicious and more importantly, meals that your whole family will love, while giving you the first chance to learn how to eat to live, not continue living to eat.

Food, as a rule, should never be a reward, it should be rewarding. That's why in these pages, I have shared my love of cooking with you and the secret to making not just good food, but great meals, giving you a chance to again eat better to live better.

I want this book to be a spring board to what you can whip up in the kitchen. You now have a choice beyond eating in and eating out. It is as close as your fingertips as you turn the pages in this book.

Remember that this is a cookbook reference guide, and just like any cookbook, it is not a Bible to be strictly adhered to. So feel free to be inspired by it and even use this guide as a reference when you are using other cookbooks. I won't mind. That is what it is made for. What I would like more than anything is for you to start eating at home more.

It doesn't matter whether you are a beginner in the kitchen or a seasoned chef. So go ahead and use this guide when you are whipping up your next pasta dish. Just look at the section on how to cook the perfect pasta. Use it when you are preparing that next roasted chicken; I will show you the right temperature to cook that chicken at.

With a little know how that I will teach you, you are about to be so surprised by how making a few easy, healthy changes can remove the temptation to leave your eating habits up to strangers by eating out all the time. You owe that much to yourself and your family. I am going to show you how and if the roles were reversed, I know you would do the same thing for me.

So again, it no longer matters whether it's a hectic weeknight, a casual brunch, or an important holiday. Family meals no longer have to be reserved for special occasions. Family meals can happen any time of day, any day of the week! You can now make it happen!

That's because family meals planned, prepared and shared together at home tend to be healthier and more balanced than meals eaten at restaurants or on the go, which is better for you.

If you are a parent, you will be thrilled to learn that young adults who were raised eating regular family meals consume more fruits, vegetables and dairy products. (So, there is hope yet for your teenagers!)

There is also an association between family meal frequency and lower rates of obesity, which is good for everyone. Isn't it time to make family meals a habit in your home again?

Before we start, just remember that if you are cooking for a family, you already know that each person will have different calorie needs, but with "Conquer Your Kitchen" you can finally cook the same nutritious foods, but vary it by portion size. For example, your hungry teenage son can eat the same meal as your picky eating five year old, he will just eat more of it.

Speaking of picky eaters, we all know one, they come in every shape and size. Just remember the rule when introducing your family to new foods, always let them start with a "no thank you" bite. Give them a little and let them try it and decide if they want more.

With that in mind, let's begin…

Mise En Place...

Where Most Home Chefs And Diets Go Wrong

If you are like me, when you want to try a new a recipe, you

often jump in without properly preparing everything that you need. It is at this point that your meals often go wrong and you find yourself ordering pizza or Chinese takeout.

Remember that all it takes is an extra 200 calories in your diet to move your scale in the wrong direction. When you cook at home, you are placing your meal in the hands of somebody that cares about what you eat...you!

Believe it or not, getting a great meal on the table quickly and effortlessly isn't just about talent or experience. The real secret to increasing your efficiency and success in the kitchen is to commit to some old fashioned planning and organization in the form of "mise en place."

What is "mise en place?" "Mise en place" (pronounced MEEZ ahn plahs) is a French culinary term that means "to put in place." The purpose of *mise en place* is to have all of your ingredients prepared and ready to go **before** you start cooking, so you don't have to stop during the cooking process to do anything other than add the next ingredient.

The key to a great meal has always been to be ready. It is no different than deciding what you want to wear the day before. Mise en place is the key to a great meal that all great chefs and home cooks, excuse me, home chefs live by.

How To Get Started

There are two simple steps when it comes to *mise en place*:

Planning:

That is the simple task of making sure you have all of the ingredients (and necessary tools) called for in a recipe before you get started.

Organizing:

That is the simple task of making sure you have all of the ingredients prepared (ready to go) before you start cooking.

Here's How:

The only way to ensure that you have all of the ingredients on hand to make a recipe is to practice the time-saving and money-saving strategy of meal planning.

Meal planning is actually the highest form of mise en place. It is the same as mapping out your day or even turning on your GPS in your car to ensure that you get to your proper location.

Again, meal planning not only guarantees that you'll have all of the ingredients necessary to execute every recipe on your meal plan, but it also helps to save time, stress and money because you've already pre-planned what you'll be cooking for the week.

Next, organize your ingredients in the order that you will need them onto the table or counter. This is no different than packing a suit case. When was the last time that you just threw everything into a bag and took off for the airport? If you have, trying to replace those missing socks is like wasting possibly an hour trying to run out to the market because you don't have milk.

Planning and prepping ahead is even a great job for your little ones, your children, who are always asking you can they help! Let them get items that are safe to retrieve for you. Then, gather up all of the ingredients, as well as all of the measuring tools and cooking tools and even the right pots and pans that are needed to carry out the recipes and put them within arm's reach.

Dice, chop, grate, mince, etc. all of the ingredients needed for whatever you are cooking so they're all ready to go *before* you start cooking.

I always find it helpful to pre-measure any ingredients in individual prep bowls or measuring cups that you can pick up from a dollar store or discount retailer. Another idea is to put them in one bowl, if you're going to add them at the same time to a recipe.

You don't have to measure out everything, just those ingredients that would cause you to take your eye off of what you are doing. For example, if a recipe calls for you to sauté garlic or onions, when you are ready to sauté the garlic or onions is not a good time to start chopping or mincing them.

My grandmother always says that if you have just a box and a bed, you should always keep it clean. So in the kitchen, my rule is to clean as I go. I keep a bowl nearby to toss trash, such as egg shells in as I go.

With less mess, the clean up after cooking is another time wasting event that you should avoid at all cost. Not only will your kitchen be neat and clean by the time your guests do arrive, but you can truly relax after your meal knowing you aren't going to be on your feet for a few more hours trying to clean up the mess that you made earlier.

With time always being of the essence, I suggest that you always focus on the items that take the longest first. Then, and only then, can you work your way towards the dishes that need less time or attention. With good timing, everything can be ready at the same time.

When it comes to holiday events, days like Thanksgiving, Christmas or the Fourth of July is not the day to start cooking. I start preparing my turkey at least two days before Thanksgiving to ensure that my turkey is the best that it can be. I hate dry turkey that you have to literally bathe in gravy to enjoy it and you should too.

With that in mind, it is okay when you have some time to schedule a prep day. You can even do this when you are planning your meals. You can spend this prep day by cleaning and seasoning your meats. You can even clean, season and separate your meat the same day that you buy them. This really helps because all you are left to do is to thaw and cook your meal.

You can chop, mince or dice any veggies that you might need, and then, pop them into the freezer, so that you can still provide healthy home cooked meals even on the busiest of days. I do this all the time, especially onions and peppers.

Last, but not least, let us talk about a home chef's worst enemy—preheating. There is a serious reason why a recipe calls for preheating; it helps ensure that food cooks properly.

Similarly, before you sauté anything, make sure that your pan is well heated. By allowing time for your pans to heat up before cooking, you'll help to ensure better, tastier results. This helps even when searing steaks, it helps lock in the juices.

Always remember, when cooking with any oil, it should be close to its smoking point before you add your recipe ingredients for best results. Be careful not to burn it.

Also, before you put those homemade cookies or muffins in the oven, be sure that your oven is preheated to the precise baking temperature called for in the recipe. You may end up with burned or scorched cookies, pies and cakes.

In the end, by remembering that putting in the necessary time upfront to plan your meals, and then, gather and prep all of the recipe's ingredients in advance, helps to ensure that the time you spend cooking is that much more efficient and enjoyable. The results will always be a healthy and delicious meal for you and/or your family and friends.

What Every Home Chef's Kitchen Needs...

Now that I have introduced you to the most important steps in your home when it comes to healthy eating, you should

know there are other things that you need to make this happen.

Just like a plumber needs tools, so does a good home cook. Or, as I like to call home cooks these days, home chefs.

It doesn't matter if you are ready to move into your new place or you have been living in your home for years, eventually, you will have to eat. Eventually, you will get tired of having a set of menus from all of the local take-out places; especially when this menu collection can start a small fire because you have so many.

Since eventually you are going to need a pot, a pan or a plate, here is a helpful set of hints on bringing your kitchen together. While I could have given you a deluxe list of kitchen gadgets, let's start with the basics, especially when you are short on space.

You can get most of this stuff at your nearest dollar or discount store. Then, when you are ready, that fancy four slice toaster can be your special treat. Remember that this is not a complete list. Feel free to add to it. Let us get started...

- Baking pans, different sizes
- Baking dishes, different sizes
- Cereal bowls

- Serving bowls
- Bottle opener
- Cake Pans, two
- Can opener
- Coffee maker
- Colander
- Crock Pot or Slow Cooker
- Cutting board
- Dish cloths
- Dish towels
- Drinking glasses
- Fluted cake pan
- Funnels
- Garlic press
- Glasses, water
- Glasses, wine
- Grater
- Juice glasses
- Ice cream scoop
- Kitchen timer
- Knives, butter
- Knife, large cutting
- Knife, small cutting
- Knife, bread
- Ladle
- Meat thermometer
- Measuring cup, set for measuring dry goods like flour
- Measuring cups, set for measuring liquids
- Measuring spoons, set
- Mixing bowl, large
- Mixer, electric
- Mugs, coffee
- Oven mitts, two
- Pan with lid, non-stick, 12 inch
- Pie dish
- Pie server

- Pizza cutter
- Pizza pan
- Plates 9 inches or 10 inches in diameter, 4-8
- Plates, dessert/bread, 4-8
- Pot with lid, medium
- Pot with lid, large
- Potato peeler
- Rolling pin
- Roasting pan
- Scissors
- Spatula, non-stick
- Storage container plastic with tight fitting lid
- Tea kettle
- Thermos
- Toaster
- Trash can
- Serving spoons, slotted and non-slotted
- Serving dishes
- Small individual serving bowls
- Toaster oven
- Utensils, teaspoons
- Utensils, tablespoons
- Utensils, forks
- Utensils, steak knives
- Whisk

The Most Important Thing In Your Home...

Have you ever noticed that when you eat in some restaurants, the plates are so big that the servers often have a hard time finding room to comfortably fit everything on the table? Or are your plates at home so big that you struggle to fit them into the sink or dish washer.

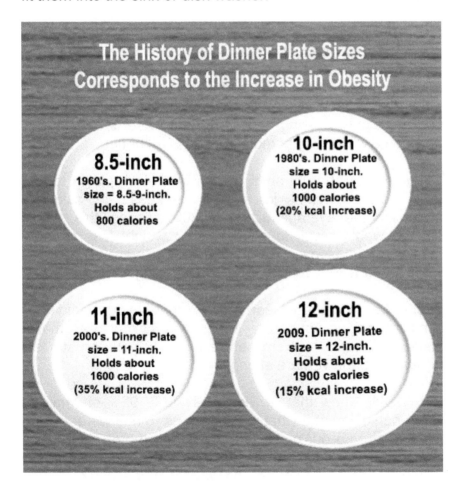

The History of Dinner Plate Sizes Corresponds to the Increase in Obesity

8.5-inch
1960's. Dinner Plate size = 8.5-9-inch.
Holds about 800 calories

10-inch
1980's. Dinner Plate size = 10-inch.
Holds about 1000 calories
(20% kcal increase)

11-inch
2000's. Dinner Plate size = 11-inch.
Holds about 1600 calories
(35% kcal increase)

12-inch
2009. Dinner Plate size = 12-inch.
Holds about 1900 calories
(15% kcal increase)

When it comes to eating less, and if you read my number one bestselling book, "The Hungry Chick Dieting Solution, you already know what millions of smart people like you already know...the size of your plate is severely affecting how you and your family eat.

Many people have often told you that using a smaller plate helps you to lose weight, but very few have ever tried to explain why and/or how, even though, researchers have long known that a simple way to cut calories is to use a smaller plate. It is just that simple.

Since the 1960s, the average plate size has increased by over 33% and so have our portion sizes. Food from the 1960s would look lost on a plate today. But, nowadays, we have to feed both our eyes and our stomachs. Since we are creatures of habit, did you know that by using a large plate, you are secretly telling your body that more is better? But, how come when we eat more we don't feel better.

Did you know that by shifting from a 12–inch plates to 10–inch plates resulted in a 22% decrease in calories? Assuming the average dinner is 800 calories, this simple change would result in an estimated weight loss of more than 10 pounds over the course of one year. That is 10 whole pounds that you can and will be losing.

That is why you should learn how to control your portions by simply changing your plate. When you switch to a smaller plate, you switch to a smaller serving and you can still feel full even though you are eating less.

You should know that we eat on average 92% of what we serve ourselves and what is given to us. Since we are piling more food onto our plates, we are eating more. Think, for a minute, about family and friends who eat at your house, do they ever accuse you of serving way too much food?

If they don't have the heart to tell you, think about how many times that they couldn't even finish what you cooked or asked to take it home. Even then, do you realize just how guilty most of us feel when we don't finish all of our food? Remember, your stomach is about the size of your fist. With a smaller plate, you can still eat what you want and you no longer have to worry about cleaning your plate ever again.

Studies have shown that people still feel satisfied when they use smaller plates. My suggestion, don't go too small though. You might be tempted to go back for seconds or thirds. You see while studies have proven over and over again that smaller plates lead to smaller portions the reason for this reduction had been unknown until recently.

Right now, I know that no one has ever explained it to you, the exact science behind it all, so allow me to do it for you right now. You see, it has been discovered that smaller plates cause us to eat less thanks to a powerful optical illusion known as the Delboeuf (pronounced del-boof) Illusion. The illusion works because we think things are smaller when we compare them to things that are larger.

For example, if you put a small piece of food on a large plate, your mind will tell you that you are eating a small portion and you will automatically put more food on the plate. However, if you put that same piece of food on a small plate, your mind will tell you that you are eating a large portion and you'll stop adding food.

It's like an empty room. We can't deal with a lot of empty space, so no matter how much we clean it out, we find ourselves filling it back up with things that we don't need. Your mind works the same way and can actually feel satisfied when you eat using a smaller plate full of food compared to a large plate with the same amount.

Let me explain this a bit more... This difference, in relative size perception, is known as the Delboeuf (pronounced again... del-boof) Illusion. It was named for the Belgian philosopher, Joseph Remi Leopold Delboeuf created it sometime between 1887 and 1888.

Right now, let's pretend that these circles are plates, with the one on the left being a 12 inch plate and the one on the right being 9- or 10-inches (in diameter or the length across the plate):

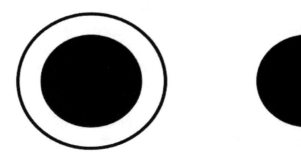

If the two black circles represent the amount of food space that you should use for your food, you should know that they are the exact same size. However, the one on the left seems larger because of the ring and will force you to add more food that you really don't need to your plate.

Do you realize that trying to force a small portion of food on a large plate will drain your willpower and motivation to eat less and more healthier? From a psychological standpoint, you are making yourself feels like you are depriving yourself. Meanwhile, the same portion feels bigger and more filling when you see it on a small plate. Use the smaller plate!

The Delboeuf Illusion has been proven to work for a wide range of plate shapes, including squares, rectangles, and triangles. In other words, it doesn't matter what you're eating, your mind will still play tricks on you when it comes to the relative size perception of your portion and your plate size.

So, forget about willpower and motivation and let your plate control your portions for you. You can safely and happily eat a full plate of food and still feel full, just start with a smaller plate. It is the same foods that you love, just a smaller plate.

Second, the size of your plate isn't the only thing that determines how much you eat. The color of your plate matters too. From research, I have learned that when the color of a person's plate matched the color of their food, they served themselves almost 30% more. That's 30% more calories that you don't need.

In other words, if you ate pasta with red tomato sauce on a dark red plate, you ate almost 30% more than you would if you had used a white plate. The same is true for eating pasta with a white Alfredo sauce on a white plate compared to a dark red plate.

The reason behind this drastic difference in serving size is that when the color of your food blends in with the color of your plate, then the amount of food doesn't appear to be as large. The result is that you will end up scooping more food onto the plate than you really need.

The higher contrast in plate color to food color will automatically prevent you from throwing an extra scoop onto the plate. When I buy plates, I tend to buy them with a color contrasting ring and simply keep my servings in the circle.

Typically, plate colors isn't something that you will think about, but changing the color of them will help your mind realize that you don't need another serving. You don't have to rely on motivation because the color of the plate is helping your mind make the decision for you. Allow it to. This will save you a lot of time and guessing when it comes to counting calories. Less food means fewer calories...

Meal Planning 101...

Contrary to popular belief, meal planning doesn't have to be about eating the same things all the time. Nor do you have to turn into a four star chef at the drop of a dime.

If anything, meal planning simply takes a lot of guess work out of the age old question... "What's for dinner?"

All too often, we find ourselves staring blankly at a clump of meat that we were supposed to make, sitting in the back of our freezer.

Or, we are turning up our nose at some food that went bad in the back of our refrigerator and we didn't even know how long it has been there. The answer to these problems is simple as planning what you are going to eat and shopping for that meal.

Meal planning isn't hard. It is simple as deciding what you want to eat, and then, making a list of the things to make it happen. But you should remember that it is impossible to plan your menu without any inspiration, so I have loaded this book with recipes, menu ideas and great tips to help you.

You will no longer panic when the clock strikes 4 P.M. and you don't have a clue as to what you are going to cook. With a little time and patience, you will be eating better because you personally know the chef.

With meal planning, this little step will eventually be guaranteed to save you time, money and frustration felt by working people all over the world. But first, I need to share a few things with you…

Here's Why You Should Always Plan Your Meals…

- Meal planning is simply about being smart and savvy to make the most of your food budget and ease the stress of your life.

- When you start, keep it simple. Stick with what works for you and/or your family and you'll have success.

- Planning your meals ensures that you are only selecting well-balanced meals.

- You will never end up with carb heavy meals or meals that go overboard on red meat. You will pay more attention to your actual meal and its different components

- Remember when planning each grain portion, you have to be aware that they aren't just talking about rice, potatoes and pasta. Consider even your breads.

- Also, your protein, especially red meat, should always be balanced by two servings of fruits or vegetables. A small salad (lettuce and tomatoes) will easily count as a serving.

- Your meals will be fresher because you will only buy, and then, use what you need and eat what you cook.

- You will stay within your shopping budget, which will save you money.

- You will save refrigerator and freezer space by not buying things that you "might eat." Every purchase should have a purpose or it shouldn't be bought.

- You will see that the best meals are those that offer up double the fun. Leftover roasted chicken can be used in a chicken soup or tossed over a salad.

- You will make fewer trips to the market for that "missing ingredient." Your cooking will become convenient and stress-free when you have everything.

- You can also plan easy meals or cook a double batch to freeze and simply reheat on your busy days.

- Remember meal planning is necessary even when you are eating out. Too much leaves a gut.

Quick Fixes!

If you find it hard to commit to a meal plan, you can fix it by:

- Planning meals that you've always wanted to try.

- Adding a new twist to the family favorite meal. Instead of just spaghetti, try angel hair or penne pasta.

- If you love to be inspired by your local produce market, just plan around your main source of protein (like fish or chicken) and spice it up in other ways, such as your side dishes (try jasmine rice or mashed sweet potatoes, seasoned with butter and brown sugar), ingredients (go spicier,) or even, the method of cooking (baking your meal, instead of cooking it on the stove.)

Write It Down When You Think About It!

- Simply write down the dinners (and lunches and snacks, if you wish) that you want to make using a calendar or even a plain sheet of paper divided by each day and meal.

- Jotting it down will make it easy to see that you already have a chicken meal planned, so you can swap it out with a pork number for the next night, or even, two days later to prevent eating the same thing.

- Always consider how long it will take to cook everything.

- Always consider how long you will have to store any ingredients. Do you have the freezer space or how long can you store certain items in the refrigerator?

- On the days that you know you are busy or simply tired; you will know how you will deal with those days.

- Also, consider your budget. You might not be able to afford prime rib every night, but you can probably handle a good whole chicken.

- From your meal plan, write your shopping list.

Meal Planning-Savvy Tips:

- The best way to ensure a balance in your meals is to have it all written down in front of you.

- On busy days, plan to succeed with quick meals, or slow cooked meals.

- Try for a range of proteins and veggies in your meals - with lots of colors and textures. Don't be afraid to serve broccoli with carrots.

- Expect to stick to the meal-plans around 80 to 90 percent of the time on a good week. But on a bad week, it could be more like 50 percent, or even, 20.

- Success can be attributed to making sure you've shopped and have all the ingredients ready to go and the enthusiasm to pull it off.

- You need to have a couple of lazy meal options ready to go for those days when just want to put something on the table, i.e. grilled cheese sandwiches and tomato soup.

This really does make life a lot simpler. And don't we all want that for our lives? I know that I do.

Creating Your Plate...

Now that you know about smaller plates, how their color matters and more about meal planning, here is another simple and effective method for losing weight, maintaining your weight loss or just eating healthier. It is called creating your plate.

 Creating your plate lets you still choose the foods you want, but changes the portion sizes so that you are getting larger portions of non-starchy vegetables and a smaller portion of starchy foods. Then, when you are ready, you can try new foods within each food category. Mix it up. Only you know what you truly love.

Creating your plate, also known as the Idaho Plate Method, is an easy way to set up healthy meals for yourself and your family. No more weighing your food, no more carrying around measuring cups and no more expensive "special foods" that taste worse than the containers that they come in. No more cooking foods that your whole family can't enjoy.

You already know that when you eat healthier, you feel better and your family eats better and feels better also. It helps them learn good eating habits for life.

You should also remember that this method of meal planning does **not** and should **not** take the place of visiting your health care professional annually for a physical or whenever a health issue arises.

Before you begin this method, make sure that you put the oversize dishes and bowls out of sight, so you do not use them ever again and the hardest part is actually over.

Now, let's look at how your plate should actually look and what you should have on each part of your plate for lunch and for dinner...

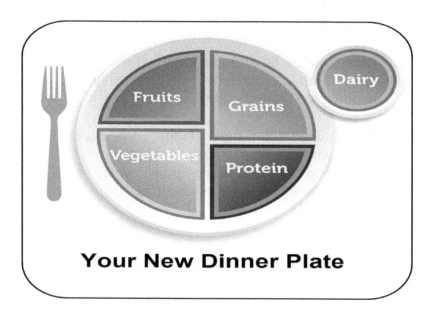

Your New Dinner Plate

Vegetables and Fruits:

- Fruits and vegetables stay on this half of the plate. This may be more vegetables than you are used to. This is okay.

- By increasing your fruits and vegetables, you are bringing your meals back into balance and adding fiber, vitamins and minerals that you might have been missing.

- Vitamins should come from your foods not a bottle. The vitamins you take are called supplements for a reason. You take them when you aren't getting enough in you daily diet (the foods that you eat.)

- Fruits and vegetables also help to fill you up without filing you out!

- It's best not to fill this half of the plate with only one kind of fruit or vegetable. You get tired of even your favorite foods that way.

- Try a small salad and use the other half of that half (or that quarter of your plate) to try a cooked vegetable so you have more variety.

- Some vegetables are higher in starch and/or carbohydrates. The vegetables that do not belong in this group includes corn, peas, yams and winter squash. Consider them as starches.

Meat/Protein...

- This should be a fourth of the plate. This is where you put your meats. You can use any type of meat, fish, poultry, tofu, eggs, and nuts. These are high in protein, but are sometimes high in fat.

- Always remove visible fat before cooking and/or eating.

- Remember, low fat foods are better for your heart and your waistline.

- Healthier cooking choices include baked, broiled and boiled items with little fat added.

- Healthier fats can be found in fish such as salmon and mackerel, and nuts (except coconut).

- Your protein portion should never be bigger than a deck of cards, unless it is a bone-in chicken.

Breads/Starches/Grains...

- This fourth of the plate is where your breads, starches and grains stay. You can eat a variety of foods in this group. Examples are noodles, rice, bread, cereal, crackers, small tortillas, potatoes, and dried beans (chili).
- For cereal and soups, use the small bowl, it fits right on this fourth of the plate.
- Some vegetables are higher in starch/carbohydrates. The vegetables again that belong in this group include corn, peas, yams, and winter squash.

Milk...

- Find a small coffee cup or glass that holds about 1 cup, or 8 ounces, for foods in this section.... fat free milk, skim milk, 1% milk, and light yogurt are your best choices.
- Calcium from milk products can help control blood pressure and helps you lose weight easier.
- Calcium is also important for strong bones.
- Use a small dish for servings of light ice cream and sugar-free pudding to add variety.
- You will need 3 servings per day from this group to get enough calcium.
- Teens and adolescents need at least 4 servings for strong bones and teeth.
- If you do not drink milk or are lactose intolerant, talk to your doctor about ways to add calcium to your diet.

Fruit...

- A serving of fruit is one small piece, like a small apple or small orange.

- Cut up any fruit (like apples) to make it more ready to eat.

- Use your small dish to hold fresh fruit substitutes like applesauce and fruit cocktail.

- Smaller dishes hold a half cup of anything.

- When using canned fruit, lite-packed and juice-packed are the best choices.

- Juice servings should be about a half of a small coffee cup or a juicing glass.

- Remember, juice does not fill you up. You will feel fuller if you eat a small orange instead of drinking the juice.

- Some fruits have less starch/carbohydrates, so you can eat a little more of them. These bonus foods are melons and berries; use your small bowl for the right serving size.

The goal with meal planning is to not dig your own grave with your own knife and fork. The most important thing for your good health and that of your family is what you put on the end of your forks. Again, you must eat better to live better. When you eat better, you will always feel better.

I Know That You Still Have Questions...

What about breakfast...

Well, it is the same situation, you can set up your breakfast  plate, or even, your lunch plate, the same way that you set up your dinner plate. You use a fourth of the plate for your meat or protein.

A fourth of your plate is for breads, starches, and grains. A dish of fruit, any kind that you want, should be included and a serving of milk.

Milk, fruits, breads, starches and grains... all affect your blood sugar levels about the same amount. That is why these foods can be traded for one another. So, if you do not want fruit for lunch, you could have another serving of milk.

Remember it is best not to skip a food group. You need the nutrients from each food group to stay healthy.

A diet low in fruits and whole grains is also low in fiber and many vitamins and minerals. You cannot trade meat and vegetable servings

How to set up a breakfast meal...

- You can choose to put any meat or protein that you want on a fourth of the plate for meat. (Try low salt foods.)

- Any breads/starches/grains food you want goes on a fourth of the plate. (always try whole grain products.)

- Any fruit that you choose goes in the small dish.

- Any milk serving goes in the milk section or simply counts as a beverage.

What about snacks...

- Plan on saving the fruit serving at meals and have it later between meals as a snack.

What about desserts...

- You can trade your fruit serving for a SMALL dessert using the small dish. Be careful though! Trading too many of your fruits for desserts can cause weight gain and poor nutrition.

What if you are not a big eater...

- You do not need to fill the entire parts of the plate.

- Remember the key is to always be consistent.

- Eat about the same amount of food on each section of the plate at each meal.

- If you have your favorite mashed potatoes one day, you should not have more on that section of your plate than the day when you have plain noodles. This will help you even out your blood sugars.

- For very small eaters and children, try to still eat a fourth of your plate in vegetables.

- Children, especially active ones, may need an extra snack of fruit or bread and milk between meals.

What if your spouse or teen-aged child tends to eat more...

- For men, add an extra bread, starch or grain serving at each meal.
- Just use a second small dish like you use for fruits for the extra bread, starch or grain serving.
- You can add the extra serving between meals as a snack.
- Your doctor or a trained dietitian can help you tailor their diet to their exact needs.

What if you tend to eat more meat than what I am suggesting...

- Yes, most people eat more protein and fat than we need.
- By using only a fourth of your plate for meat, you can lower your weight and cholesterol. Remember, it's the healthy thing to do.
- A portion should never be bigger than a deck of cards.

What about eating out...

- When eating out, simply order smaller servings and follow the same plate set up.
- Fill a to-go box with the extra food items <u>before</u> you begin your meal. It makes it easier to avoid over eating. You can create another meal or snack with it.
- Salad bars are a great way to get your vegetables but make sure to limit those foods with lots of mayonnaise or dressings, like ranch or blue cheese dressing.

- Remember potato salad and macaroni salad goes on the Breads/Starches/Grains section of your plate, not the Vegetable portion.

What about fats like margarine, salad dressings, whipped cream, sour cream and cooking sprays...

- Try to use less! Be skimpy
- Mayonnaise, try light or fat free mayonnaise.
- Try light salad dressings or fat free and always add on the side, even at home.
- Sour Cream, try light or fat free.
- Cooking spray, always count 1, 2, 3, and then, stop spraying. That's it.
- Gravy, try light or fat free broth and always be skimpy and serve in a small side dish.
- When making homemade, skim the fat off the meat broth.
- Your doctor should check your cholesterol at least once a year and follow your doctor's advice to lower your cholesterol.

What are the best ways to cook meat...

- Grilled
- Broiled
- Baked
- Boiled
- Saute, in light oils
- Steamed

Limit these methods...

- Fried
- Breaded, especially when fried
- With heavy sauces

What else can you do…

- Make sure the food stacked the highest on the plate is the vegetables.
- Do not let the foods touch each other. Example: my meat cannot touch my mashed potatoes.
- By not letting your food touch, you make the serving size of foods slightly smaller.
- Activity helps you use up more energy, which helps you lose weight.
- If you spend an afternoon working in the garden you will burn more calories and this extra activity will help you lose weight.
- Daily activity is recommended for everyone.
- Talk to your doctor before starting any exercise program.
- Remember to always start slow.

If you have little activity in your day, start with something easy (weather and safety permitting)…

- Day 1: Try 5 minutes of walking after one meal.
- Day 2: Increase to 10 minutes after one meal.
- Day 3: Increase to 15 minutes after each meal.
- Day 4: Try 20 minutes after each meal.
- Day 5: Increase to 30 minutes after each meal.

If you are sore afterwards, stay at the same time you did the day before until you feel you can advance to the next level.

If you have been inactive for a long time, just moving around a room will help you. The goal is to get your blood flowing and your heart beating. The goal is to burn off the calories from what you just ate. You don't want to spend the rest of your night in front of the television.

Doing the dishes and tidying up around the house may be a good workout for you. Remember to start slow though. When you have more time, try a new activity with a friend, walking, exercise class, or water aerobics. Make it fun!

Remember to reward yourself for your extra effort. (Not with food though.) A night at the movies or a new trinket, if you have been active for 7 days can be a fun thing to look forward to. This has always worked for me. Try it.

Drinking Water 101...

Let's talk about water for a few minutes. This is typically the  one part of people's meals that they stop thinking about once the meal is actually cooked and ready to be served. When it comes to water, this might be the most important part of your meal.

This is the reason why it is given to you in every restaurant before your meal is even served. Best of all, it doesn't have any calories at all.

So let's begin with a simple question... How much water do you actually drink during the day? A cup disguised as your morning coffee? Did you drink a soda at lunch? Did you have a glass of juice at dinner? Soda, juice, and coffee, sure it's a liquid but, it's not the one thing that your body really needs—actual water.

The truth is the only time that most of us see actual water is on the table before a meal at a restaurant. Often, we don't even drink that. We just don't drink enough water, which our body needs for good health, even though we know that it is good for us.

It is estimated that 75% of all Americans are dehydrated. That's over 200 million people, not just you. The problem is most people often mistake thirst for hunger and they will eat something faster than they will drink something. This is the biggest dieting mistake that most people make every single day, even if you are trying to lose weight or not.

Water actually regulates your body temperature, removes waste, transports nutrients to cells, cushions joints and protects your vital organs, restores the fluids lost by perspiration and other natural body functions.

Water helps flush out unnecessary waste products, salts and toxins from our bodies. Without water, your body doesn't stand a chance to function properly.

If you intend to lose weight, you should already be drinking enough water every day anyway. How much you ask? You should know that it isn't the eight to ten glasses that everybody thinks. This amount actually varies from person to person based on your actual weight. To find out how much, take your actual body weight and divide it by two. Go ahead. I will wait for you. (Smiling.)

The result is your water number or how much water in ounces, preferably filtered water, which removes a lot of toxins that are found in local tap water, which you will need to drink in order to maintain good health.

For example, let's say that you weigh 120 pounds. Divide that by two and you will get 60 ounces. Those 60 ounces, divided by 8 which is the number of ounces in a cup, is about the 7 and a half cups of water or more that you need to drink, especially if you have a very active lifestyle, or if you sweat a lot.

You should know that drinking water is also the best way to fight back against bloating and unnecessary water weight gain, which is caused by your body attempting to hold on to every bit of water that it can get.

Bloating is already a sure sign that you simply aren't drinking enough water and you have too much salt in your body. That's because salt also leeches water from the body, which only leads to further dehydration, bloating and water weight gain.

This is also important news for women, who suffer from monthly menstrual bloating. This kind of bloating usually starts a week before your cycle starts when you may be craving chocolate, chips and other sugary or salty snacks. This is the time that you should avoid them the most and drink more water. It will help with your cramps as well.

In any situation, try to think of water as your most important food group. The key is to take the time to drink enough of it. The problem is that many people will reach for a soda to quench their thirst or as a pick me up. That caffeine often will only make you feel even thirstier.

Did you know that by replacing just one of these sodas a day with water, you can significantly reduce your caloric intake on any given day? Imagine the results of you replacing just two sodas a day with two glasses of ice cold water.

You should also know that thirst is the number one cause of afternoon fatigue, which causes your body to work harder to pump blood through your system, causing severe headaches. So, use whatever excuse that you can to drink more water.

Carry a bottle with you that you can quickly refill to make sure that you are drinking enough water, and then, do it. Drink more water.

You should also drink water like this all year long. Some people think you only need to drink water like this when the weather is hot. You need to drink water like this even in the winter. The number one sign of dehydration in winter is dry skin, fatigue and cracked lips.

Also, don't be afraid to revisit your water number as you lose weight. The less that you weigh, the less water that you will need. In any situation, also make sure that you do not to overdo it.

Drinking too much water can cause other problems. That's because it lowers the body's natural sodium levels that the body needs, which can shut down a person's kidneys and prove to be fatal.

People instead should stick to drinking less than four glasses of water an hour. That's all that a person's kidneys can actually handle. You can always get a water bottle and mark a certain time to drink a certain amount on the outside of it using a permanent marker.

Right now, now that we are talking about calories, shouldn't we take a moment to talk about the most dreaded word in weight management... calories.

Eating the Right Amount of Calories 101...

Everyone has a personal calorie limit. Staying within yours can help you get to or maintain a healthy weight. Reaching a healthier weight is a balancing act. The secret is learning how to balance your "energy in" and "energy out" over the long run. "Energy in" is the calories from foods and beverages you have each day. "Energy out" is the calories you burn for basic body functions and physical activity.

Where Is Your Energy Balance...

Maintaining weight — Your weight will stay the same when the calories you eat and drink equal the calories you burn.

Losing weight — You will lose weight when the calories you eat and drink are less than the calories you burn.

Gaining weight — You will gain weight when the calories you eat and drink are greater than the calories you burn.

The current high rates of overweight and obesity in the United States mean that many people are taking in more calories than they burn.

Recommended Daily Caloric Intake...

Have you ever wondered how many calories you need a day to maintain your current weight? Though this is based on a variety of factors, the USDA assigns individuals to a calorie level based on gender, age and activity level.

The following chart can serve as a general guide to help you determine how many calories you need a day if you are trying to find your energy balance and lose weight or maintain your weight loss.

43

Gender	Age (years)	Sedentary[b]	Moderately Active[c]	Active[d]
Child	2-3	1,000	1,000-1,400	1,000-1,400
Female	4-8	1,200	1,400-1,600	1,400-1,800
	9-13	1,600	1,600-2,000	1,800-2,200
	14-18	1,800	2,000	2,400
	19-30	2,000	2,000-2,200	2,400
	31-50	1,800	2,000	2,200
	51+	1,600	1,800	2,000-2,200
Male	4-8	1,400	1,400-1,600	1,600-2,000
	9-13	1,800	1,800-2,200	2,000-2,600
	14-18	2,200	2,400-2,800	2,800-3,200
	19-30	2,400	2,600-2,800	3,000
	31-50	2,200	2,400-2,600	2,800-3,000
	51+	2,000	2,200-2,400	2,400-2,800

Please note that this chart is meant to be an estimate only, and is intended for the average adult, within a healthy body weight range, who wants to maintain their weight.

Actual calories needed to maintain weight may vary based on muscle mass, activity and a variety of other factors. For example, if you are overweight or underweight, your daily caloric needs may differ from the calories listed on this guide.

Weight loss requires burning off more calories than you consume through exercise. Please consult with a health care professional to determine how many calories you need to reach your desired goal. Be sure to mention and discuss your activity levels with your doctor.

What Are The Activity Levels...

Sedentary or Inactive (b): You have a sedentary activity level if you are inactive and perform less than 30 minutes of moderate physical activity each day in addition to regular daily activities, like work.

Moderate (c): To achieve a moderate activity level, you perform at least 30 minutes and up to 60 minutes a day of moderate physical activity in addition to daily activities.

Active (d): To achieve the active level, you perform 60 or more minutes of moderate physical activity each day in addition to daily activities.

Getting Started...

- Keep your calorie limit in mind when deciding what to eat and drink. For example, if your calorie limit is 2,000 calories per day, think about how those calories can be split up among meals, snacks, and beverages over the course of a day.

- Your meals and beverages doesn't have to be the same type of food or size each day. If you eat a larger lunch, think about eating a smaller meal at dinner.

- Compare food and beverage options and think about how they fit within your calorie limit. For example, a snack with 200 calories may be a better option than another with 500 calories.

- Use your daily calorie limit to help you decide which foods and drinks to choose.

- For a healthier you, use the Nutrition Facts label to make smart food choices quickly and easily.

- Check the label of similar products for calories, and choose the foods and drinks with fewer calories.

- Be sure to look at the serving size and how many servings you are actually consuming, as well. If you eat twice the serving size, you double the calories.

- When eating out, calorie information may be available on menus, in a pamphlet, or online.

How To Read Even Your Basic Food Labels...

People look at food labels for different reasons. But whatever the reason, many consumers would like to know how to use this information more effectively and easily.

The following label-building skills are intended to make it easier for you to use nutrition labels to make quick, informed food choices that contribute to a healthy diet. It also allows you to count potential harmful chemicals in many foods, in addition to calories.

The information in the main or top section (see #1-4 and #6 on the sample nutrition label below), can vary with each food product; it contains product-specific information (serving size, calories, and nutrient information).

The bottom part (see #5 on the sample label) contains a footnote with Daily Values (DVs) for 2,000 and 2,500 calorie diets.

This footnote provides recommended dietary information for important nutrients, including fats, sodium and fiber. The footnote is found only on larger packages and does not change from product to product.

In the following Nutrition Facts label, you will find certain sections colored to help you focus on those areas, which will be explained in detail. You will not see these colors on the food labels on products like this when you purchase them.

Sample Label for Macaroni and Cheese

Nutrition Facts

Serving Size 1 cup (228g)
Servings Per Container 2

(1) **Start Here** ➡

Amount Per Serving

Calories 250   Calories from Fat 110

(2) **Check Calories**

	% Daily Value*
Total Fat 12g	**18%**
Saturated Fat 3g	**15%**
Trans Fat 3g	
Cholesterol 30mg	**10%**
Sodium 470mg	**20%**
Total Carbohydrate 31g	**10%**

(3) **Limit these Nutrients**

(6)

Quick Guide to % DV

Dietary Fiber 0g	**0%**
Sugars 5g	
Protein 5g	
Vitamin A	**4%**
Vitamin C	**2%**
Calcium	**20%**
Iron	**4%**

• **5% or less is Low**

• **20% or more is High**

(4) **Get Enough of these Nutrients**

---

* Percent Daily Values are based on a 2,000 calorie diet. Your Daily Values may be higher or lower depending on your calorie needs.

	Calories:	2,000	2,500
Total Fat	Less than	65g	80g
Sat Fat	Less than	20g	25g
Cholesterol	Less than	300mg	300mg
Sodium	Less than	2,400mg	2,400mg
Total Carbohydrate		300g	375g
Dietary Fiber		25g	30g

(5) **Footnote**

Calorie Counting 101...

Right now, at this point, it doesn't matter if you have lost or is currently losing weight using my book, The Hungry Chick Dieting Solution, or another diet plan or weight loss program, your number one goal is to maintain that weight loss. Let's start with the basics...calories.

People hate calories because they remind us of how much work we have to do to burn off a few moments of pleasure that some unhealthy foods bring.

Some programs will tell you that you shouldn't count calories or even worry about the foods that you eat. But, I have always stressed that it isn't about what you eat, but how much and what you do afterwards with that fuel that you just received.

It's good to know how many calories that you are consuming whether you are on a diet or just making sure that you are eating enough to stay healthy. The problem is that packaged foods often tell us how many calories comes in that box or package, but what about other foods?

That's why I have put together a list of several common foods and how many calories that you can expect to find in each serving or portion. This way you can keep track of your caloric intake every day.

A calorie is something that you need to be aware of as you lose weight. The slimmer your body, the fewer calories that you will eventually need to maintain that weight. Also, you should also never feel hungry again.

Also, if you decide to have a beer (144 calories) with your co-workers or friends after work, you won't should not beat yourself up for it. It simply means that you will have to be inspired to work it off some other way. Go do the dishes or some laundry, which actually helps to burn off calories! Yes, doing dishes and laundry helps.

Also remember that there are a lot of great low calorie substitutes for high calorie foods, such as a chicken burger (130 calories) versus a hamburger (250 calories). You just have to look!

The goal right now is to end this love-hate relationship that most people have with counting calories in order to lose weight. You should also end this feeling that you need to always treat yourself with food. Trust me again, shoes, jewelry, new clothes, or even, getting your nails done work just as well.

You should also know that I am not going to make you even try to count every last calorie. The key is awareness about how many calories certain foods have in them. Awareness is key and awareness brings about change in how and what you eat.

If 2000 calories is all that you need, you can simply use the United Stated Department of Health And Human Services and the United States Department of Agriculture's guideline for a 2000 calorie day:

- ✓ 300-500 calorie breakfast
- ✓ 150 calorie snack
- ✓ 400-600 calorie lunch

✓ 150 calorie snack
✓ 400-600 calorie dinner

Knowing this will also help you order at many restaurants that are required to, or voluntarily, list their calories on the menu, like Subway. Also, if you know that what you are eating is over the required calories, then, eat it while drinking a glass of water. Water doesn't have any calories to add to your caloric intake.

Always remember that calories are simply a measure of energy. It is well known that in order to gain weight, more calories need to be entering your body than leaving it. If more calories leave your body than enter it, then you lose weight.

With that in mind, you have to also consider that by just cutting calories without thinking about the foods that you eat is usually not a good way to lose weight. It might work for some; most people will end up hungry and eventually give up on their diet.

That is why I recommend that you make a few other permanent changes to help you maintain a lower calorie intake in the long term, so that you won't feel so starved.

You should remember that again your calorie intake varies from person to person. What works for your sister, your Mom or even your best friend, might not work for you. For example, if you know that you should only consume 2,000 calories day, then, an eight ounce steak alone will account for about 700 calories.

Bake two lamb chops (256 calories) and have a cup of broccoli (24) with an ounce of cheddar cheese (114), pasta (100) and a cup of tea with honey (110). That's only 606 calories.

Those 606 calories sounds a lot better than one 700 calorie steak that you haven't even added a side to or a vegetable. Then, don't forget the steak sauce or your gravy. That's a lot of calories. That's calories and more calories that your body really doesn't need.

You should also know that these caloric suggestions aren't written in stone, it is okay to go slightly over your limit of a 600 calorie dinner, but, not too far though. When in doubt, don't eat it. If it is not good for you, you are not being good to you. Too much leaves a gut.

Remember that a healthy meal will keep you within your limit and on track to your ideal weight and a healthier you. At this point, with all calories, awareness is the key. Again, awareness brings about change…

Meats	Portion	Calories
Raw Beef	1 ounce	88
Raw Lean Beef	1 ounce	75
Grilled/Broiled Beef	1 ounce	107
Lamb	1 ounce	80
Lamb Chop	1 chop	128
Deer	1 ounce	42
Pepperoni	1 ounce	148
Grilled/Broiled Steak	1 ounce	51
Raw Bacon	1 ounce	150

Cooked Bacon	1 ounce	135
Ham	1 ounce	45
Pork	1 ounce	76
Pork Chop	1 ounce	75
Pork Sausage	1 patty	92
Pork Roast	1 ounce	55
Chicken Roasted	1 cup	240
Chicken Hot dog	1 full	116
Turkey	1 ounce	45
Turkey Hot dog	1 full	102
Caviar	1 ounce	72
Raw Clams	1 medium	11
Canned Clams	1 cup	237
Cod	1 ounce	25
Crab	1 ounce	30
Lobster	1 ounce	33
Raw Oyster	1 medium	8
Salmon	1 ounce	50
Canned Salmon	1 ounce	40
Raw Scallops	1 ounce	25
Shrimp	1 ounce	30
Prawns	1 ounce	30

Tuna	1 ounce	50
Canned Tuna	1 ounce	35
Vegetables	**Serving**	**Calories**
Red Pepper	1 medium	39
Green Pepper	1 medium	17
Small Potato	1 medium	88
Baked Potato	1 medium	161
Baked Sweet Potato	1 medium	136
Boiled Potato	1 medium	861
Fresh Potato	1 medium	80
Cucumber	1 medium	19
Raw Asparagus	1 ounce	8
Fresh Green Beans	1 cup	44
Canned Green Beans	1 cup	46
Beetroot	1 cup	60
Broccoli	1 cup	24
Brussels Sprouts	1 ounce	12
Raw Cabbage	1 cup	56
Corn	1 cup	132
Raw Eggplant	1 medium	27
Garlic	1 clove	4
Ginger	1 ounce	20

Saffron	1 teaspoon	2
Salt	1 teaspoon	0
Lettuce	1 head	21
Mushrooms	1 cup	20
White Onion	1 medium	40
Green Onions	1 cup	32
Canned Pumpkin	1 cup	80
Radish	1 cup	18
Raw Spinach	1 leaf	2
Tomato	1 medium	26
Fresh Green Beans	1 cup	44
Green Peas	1 cup	96
Shallots	1 tablespoon	8
Tomatillo	1 medium	11
Fruits	**Portion**	**Calories**
Apple	1 medium	80
Apricot	1 medium	17
Avocado	1 ounce	50
Banana	1 medium	105
Blackberries	1 cup	74
Blueberries	1 cup	82

Boysenberries	1 cup	82
Fresh Cherries	1 cup	100
Dried Cherries	1 cup	560
Cantaloupe	1 medium	188
Cranberries	1 cup	46
Dates	1 cup	502
Fig	1 medium	37
Dried Figs	5 figs	240
Grapes	1 cup	62
Grapefruit	1 medium	120
Kiwifruit	1 medium	46
Lemon	1 medium	17
Lime	1 medium	20
Mango	1 medium	135
Nectarine	1 medium	67
Orange	1 medium	62
Papaya	1 medium	117
Peach	1 medium	37
Pear	1 medium	100
Canned Pear	1 ounce	75
Pineapple	1 cup	78

Plum	1 ounce	16
Pomegranate	1 ounce	19
Raisins	1 cup	438
Strawberries	1 cup	46
Tangerine	1 medium	37
Watermelon	1 cup	50
Other Foods	**Portion**	**Calories**
Bread	1 slice	70
Cornflakes	1 cup	100
Cheddar Cheese	1 ounce	114
Cottage Cheese	1 cup	234
Tofu	1 ounce	22
Chocolate	1 ounce	140
White Chocolate	1 ounce	162
Dark Chocolate	1 ounce	180
Cocoa	1 cup	200
Cornstarch	1 tablespoon	30
Ketchup	1 tablespoon	15
Mayonnaise	1 tablespoon	100
Mustard	1 tablespoon	10

Olive	1 full	12
Oatmeal	1 cup	145
Chocolate Syrup	1 tablespoon	25
Yeast	1 ounce	80
Soy Sauce	1 tablespoon	11
Buttermilk	1 cup	100
Soy Milk	1 cup	80
Greek Yogurt	1 cup	140
Egg	1 full	75
Butter	1 tablespoon	100
Peanut Butter	1 tablespoon	95
Almonds	1 ounce	160
Cashews	1 ounce	160
Peanuts	1 ounce	160
Walnuts	1 ounce	140
Pistachios	1 ounce	165
Barley	1 cup	650
Noodles	1 cup	190
Cream of Tartar	1 teaspoon	2
Popcorn	1 ounce	110
Salsa	1 tablespoon	3
Pasta	1 ounce	100

Rice	1 cup	240
Brown Rice	1 cup	210
Honey	1 tablespoon	60
Maple Syrup	1 tablespoon	50

Beverage	Serving Size	Calories
Milk	1 cup	157
Beer	1 bottle	144
Gin	1 ounce	65
Rum	1 ounce	65
Vodka	1 ounce	65
Whiskey	1 ounce	65
Red Wine	1 ounce	23
White Wine	1 ounce	22
Coffee	1 cup	40
Tea	1 cup	50

Now that you are aware of the calories in certain foods, let's learn have a frank discussion about some of those basic cooking terms that tend to confuse people in other cookbooks and add more calories...

Basic Cooking Terms...

In addition to being aware of the calories, we have to make certain words a part of your everyday vocabulary: baked, boiled, broiled, dry broiled (in lemon juice or wine,) garden fresh, grilled, high fiber, in its own juice, poached, red sauce, roasted, steamed and whole grain.

Right now, let's also take the guess work out of some of the terms used in many cookbooks. These terms might be confusing or even downright unhealthy because they may be the source of hidden calories, unhealthy fats or cholesterol.

So that you are never confused by a recipe or cookbook ever again, here is help…

Al dente: Italian term used to describe pasta that is cooked until it offers a slight resistance to the bite.

Bake: To cook by dry heat, usually in the oven.

Barbecue: Usually used generally to refer to grilling done outdoors or over an open charcoal or wood fire. More specifically, barbecue refers to long, slow direct-heat cooking, including liberal basting with a barbecue sauce.

Baste: To moisten foods during cooking with pan drippings or special sauce to add flavor and prevent drying.

Batter: A mixture containing flour and liquid, thin enough to pour.

Beat: To mix rapidly in order to make a mixture smooth and light by incorporating as much air as possible.

Blanch: To immerse in rapidly boiling water and allow to cook slightly.

Blend: To incorporate two or more ingredients thoroughly.

Boil: To heat a liquid until bubbles break continually on the surface.

Broil: To cook on a grill under strong, direct heat.

Caramelize: To heat sugar in order to turn it brown and give it a special taste.

Chop: To cut solids into pieces with a sharp knife or other chopping device.

Clarify: To separate and remove solids from a liquid, thus making it clear.

Cream: To soften a fat, especially butter, by beating it at room temperature. Butter and sugar are often creamed together, making a smooth, soft paste.

Cure: To preserve meats by drying and salting and/or smoking.

Deglaze: To dissolve the thin glaze of juices and brown bits on the surface of a pan in which food has been fried, sautéed or roasted. To do this, add liquid and stir and scrape over high heat, thereby adding flavor to the liquid for use as a sauce.

Degrease: To remove fat from the surface of stews, soups, or stock. Usually cooled in the refrigerator so that fat hardens and is easily removed.

Dice: To cut food in small cubes of uniform size and shape.

Dissolve: To cause a dry substance to pass into solution in a liquid.

Dredge: To sprinkle or coat with flour or other fine substance.

Drizzle: To sprinkle drops of liquid lightly over food in a casual manner.

Dust: To sprinkle food with dry ingredients. Use a strainer or a jar with a perforated cover, or try the good, old-fashioned way of shaking things together in a paper bag.

Fillet: As a verb, to remove the bones from meat or fish. A fillet (or filet) is the piece of flesh after it has been boned.

Flake: To break lightly into small pieces.

Flambé: To flame foods by dousing in some form of potable alcohol and setting alight.

Fold: To incorporate a delicate substance, such as whipped cream or beaten egg whites, into another substance without releasing air bubbles. Cut down through mixture with spoon, whisk, or fork; go across bottom of bowl, up and over, close to surface. The process is repeated, while slowing rotating the bowl, until the ingredients are thoroughly blended.

Fricassee: To cook by braising; usually applied to fowl or rabbit.

Fry: To cook in hot fat. To cook in a fat is called pan-frying or sautéing; to cook in a one-to-two inch layer of hot fat is called shallow-fat frying; to cook in a deep layer of hot fat is called deep-fat frying, or simply, deep frying.

Garnish: To decorate a dish both to enhance its appearance and to provide a flavorful foil. Parsley, lemon slices, raw vegetables, chopped chives, and other herbs are all forms of garnishes.

Glaze: To cook with a thin sugar syrup cooked to crack stage; mixture may be thickened slightly. Also, to cover with a thin, glossy icing.

Grate: To rub on a grater that separates the food in various sizes of bits or shreds.

Gratin: From the French word for "crust." Term used to describe any oven-baked dish--usually cooked in a shallow oval gratin dish--on which a golden brown crust of bread crumbs, cheese or creamy sauce is form.

Grill: To cook on a grill over intense heat.

Grind: To process solids by hand or mechanically to reduce them to tiny particles.

Julienne: To cut vegetables, fruits, or cheeses into thin strips.

Knead: To work and press dough with the palms of the hands or mechanically, to develop the gluten in the flour.

Lukewarm: Neither cool nor warm; approximately body temperature.

Marinate: To flavor and moisturize pieces of meat, poultry, seafood or vegetable by soaking them in or brushing them with a liquid mixture of seasonings known as a marinade. Dry marinade mixtures composed of salt, pepper, herbs or spices may also be rubbed into meat, poultry or seafood.

Meuniere: Dredged with flour and sautéed in butter.

Mince: To cut or chop food into extremely small pieces.

Mix: To combine ingredients usually by stirring.

Pan-broil: To cook uncovered in a hot fry pan, pouring off fat as it accumulates.

Pan-fry: To cook in small amounts of fat.

Parboil: To boil until partially cooked; to blanch. Usually this procedure is followed by final cooking in a seasoned sauce.

Pare: To remove the outermost skin of a fruit or vegetable.

Peel: To remove the outer skin from vegetables or fruits.

Pickle: To preserve meats, vegetables, and fruits in brine.

Pinch: A pinch is the trifling amount you can hold between your thumb and forefinger.

Pit: To remove the large seed from fruits like peaches.

Planked: Cooked on a thick hardwood plank.

Plump: To soak dried fruits in liquid until they swell.

Poach: To cook very gently in hot liquid kept just below the boiling point.

Puree: To mash foods until perfectly smooth by hand, by rubbing through a sieve or food mill, or by whirling in a blender or food processor.

Reduce: To boil down to reduce the volume.

Refresh: To run cold water over food that has been parboiled, to stop the cooking process quickly.

Render: To make solid fat into liquid by melting it slowly.

Roast: To cook by dry heat in an oven.

Sauté: To cook and/or brown food in a small amount of hot fat.

Scald: To bring to a temperature just below the boiling point.

Scallop: To bake a food, usually in a casserole, with sauce or other liquid. Crumbs often are sprinkled over.

Score: To cut narrow grooves or gashes partway through the outer surface of food.

Sear: To brown very quickly by intense heat. This method increases shrinkage but develops flavor and improves appearance.

Shred: To cut or tear in small, long, narrow pieces.

Sift: To put one or more dry ingredients through a sieve or sifter.

Simmer: To cook slowly in liquid over low heat at a temperature of about 180°. The surface of the liquid should be barely moving, broken from time to time by slowly rising bubbles.

Skim: To remove impurities, whether scum or fat, from the surface of a liquid during cooking, thereby resulting in a clear, cleaner-tasting final produce.

Steam: To cook in steam in a pressure cooker, deep well cooker, double boiler, or a steamer made by fitting a rack in a kettle with a tight cover. A small amount of boiling water is used with more water being added during steaming process, if necessary.

Steep: To extract color, flavor, or other qualities from a substance by leaving it in water just below the boiling point.

Sterilize: To destroy microorganisms by boiling, dry heat, or steam.

Stew: To simmer slowly in a small amount of liquid for a long time.

Stir: To mix ingredients with a circular motion until well blended or of uniform consistency.

Toss: To combine ingredients with a lifting motion.

Truss: To secure poultry with string or skewers, to hold its shape while cooking.

Whip: To beat rapidly to incorporate air and produce expansion, as in heavy cream or egg whites.

Pantry Basics 101...

While a good shopping list is the key to a quick and painless trip to the supermarket, a well-stocked pantry is the best way to ensure that you'll have most of what you'll need to cook once you get home.

Remember that this is not a complete list. Feel free to add or remove anything based on your taste, budget, interests, allergies and/or dietary restrictions...

Oils, Vinegars and Condiments:

- Oils: canola oil, extra-virgin olive oil, toasted sesame
- Vinegars: balsamic, distilled white, red wine, rice
- Ketchup
- Mayonnaise
- Dijon mustard
- Soy sauce
- Chili paste
- Hot sauce
- Worcestershire

Seasonings:

- Kosher salt
- Black peppercorns
- Dried herbs and spices: bay leaves, cayenne pepper, crushed red pepper, cumin, ground coriander, oregano, paprika, rosemary, thyme leaves, cinnamon, cloves, allspice, ginger, nutmeg
- Spice blends: chili powder, curry powder, Italian seasoning
- Vanilla extract

Canned Goods and Bottled Items:

- Canned beans: black, cannellini, chickpeas, kidney
- Capers
- Olives
- Peanut butter
- Preserves or jelly
- Low-sodium stock or broth
- Canned tomatoes
- Tomatoes, canned and paste
- Salsa
- Tuna fish

Grains and Legumes

- Breadcrumbs: regular, panko
- Couscous
- Dried lentils
- Pasta: regular, whole wheat
- Rice: brown, jasmine, basmati
- Rolled oats
- One other dried grain: try barley, millet, quinoa or wheat berries

Baking Products

- Baking powder
- Baking soda
- Brown sugar
- Cornstarch
- All-purpose flour
- Granulated sugar
- Honey

Refrigerator Basics

- Low fat butter
- Low fat cheese: sharp cheddar, feta, Parmesan, mozzarella
- Large eggs
- 2% or skim milk
- Plain low fat yogurt
- Corn tortillas

Freezer Basics

- Frozen fruit: blackberries, blueberries, peaches, strawberries
- Frozen vegetables: broccoli, bell pepper and onion mix, corn, edamame, peas, spinach

Storage Produce

- Garlic
- Onions (red, yellow)
- Potatoes
- Dried fruit: raisins, apples, apricots
- Nuts or seeds: almonds, peanuts, sunflower

Herbs & Spices 101...

Food is always better when properly seasoned. You'll enjoy cooking a lot more once you've mastered the herb  and spice basics. You don't need to make drastic changes in your eating plan to benefit from seasonings.

Research has also shown that herbs and spices have the potential to boost metabolism, promote satiety (read: contentment), aid weight management and improve the overall quality of a diet.

If you like using fresh herbs or spices, just double the amount to get the same levels of active substances in their dried counterparts. Don't over do it, or it will leave you with a sort of residue on your foods.

With this in mind, here's how to incorporate more herbs and spices into your favorite foods...

How to Test for Freshness

- To ensure freshness, it is best to open and visually check spices and herbs annually to see if the spice or herb looks fresh.
- Green, leafy herbs will fade upon aging.
- Be aware; however, that different herbs naturally vary in color and should not always be compared against each other. For example, tarragon is naturally greener in color than rosemary.
- Additionally, some dill products contain the flower portion, giving them a more yellow color than those without the flowers.

- Red colored spices, such as paprika, red pepper and chili powder will turn from red to brown in color.

- Crush a small amount of the spice or herb in your hand and smell it. If the aroma is not rich, full and immediate, the spice or herb has probably lost much of its potency. (Exception: Whole spices, such as peppercorns and cinnamon stick, have a protective outer coating and will not release its full fragrance until broken or crushed.)

- Compare the aroma (Be aware, however, that subtle changes may also occur with each new crop.) of a freshly purchased spice or herb to that which you've stored for a year or more to see the difference.

- Spices and herbs are made up of numerous flavor components. Each component dissipates at varying rates over time, altering the overall balance of flavors in spices and herbs as they age.

- The initial quality of a spice and herb can impact its shelf life, with a higher quality product retaining its good flavor longer than a lower quality version.

How to Add:

- Spices and herbs should be used to enhance the natural flavor of food--not disguise or obscure it.

- Many herbs and spices can complement a dish and each other; however, be selective in their combinations. Avoid using too many at one time.
- Use a dry spoon to obtain the amount that you need.
- Do not sprinkle seasoning directly from the container into a steaming pot. The rising moisture may diminish the potency of the spice or herb remaining in the jar, or may cause it to clump or spoil more quickly.

- Crush leaf herbs, such as oregano, thyme or basil, in your hand before use for an immediate release of flavor when added to your meal.

When To Add:

- Herbs may be added near the end of cooking for more distinct flavor, or at the beginning for more blended flavors.
- Ground spices and herbs release their flavors readily. In long cooking dishes, such as stews, add these near the end of the cooking time to minimize the "cooking off" of its flavors.
- Whole spices and bay leaves release flavor more slowly than ground or leaf form and are ideal for using in dishes with longer cooking times.
- For easy removal after cooking, tie in cheesecloth or place in tea ball before adding to foods.

- For uncooked foods, such as salad dressings, fruits or fruit juices, add spices and herbs several hours before serving to allow flavors to develop and "marry" or blend.
- Alternatively, the liquid with the seasonings may be heated briefly to release the flavor, and then, allowed to cool.
- For salad dressings, add the spices to the vinegar and allow to stand before adding the oil.

How Much to Add:

- There is no general rule for the correct amount of spices and herbs to use--the pungency of each spice and herb differs and its effect on different foods varies.
- It is best to start with recipes that have been well tested or from a reliable source. The amounts can later be adjusted to suit and personalize individual tastes.

- When no recipe is available, try starting with 1/4 teaspoon for 4 servings, per pound of meat, or for each pint (2 cups) of sauce or soup; adjust as necessary.
- For cayenne and garlic powder, decrease to 1/8 teaspoon; adjust as necessary.
- Red pepper flavors increase in intensity upon cooking. Use in small increments to allow the flavor to intensify during cooking.

A Dozen Most Essential Spices:

Keeping your spice cabinet well-stocked is key to easier cooking and baking. In addition to salt and pepper, the following are spices, herbs and flavors recommended to keep on-hand:

- Basil
- Garlic Powder
- Minced Onion
- Chili Powder
- Ground Cinnamon
- Dill Weed
- Ground Ginger
- Oregano
- Paprika
- Rosemary
- Thyme
- Vanilla Extract

Personalize Your Pantry:

The following spices are also recommended for your pantry if you like to prepare certain types of food. Stock these in addition to your essential spices.

- Crushed red pepper
- Italian seasoning
- Cumin
- Curry powder or paste

Simplified Measurements

Let's Take The Guess Work Out Of Measurements…

3 teaspoons	= 1 tablespoon
4 tablespoons	= one-quarter cup
5 tablespoons and 1 teaspoon	= one-third cup
8 tablespoons	= one-half cup
10 tablespoons and 2 teaspoons	= two-thirds cup
12 tablespoons	= three-quarters cup
16 tablespoons	= 1 cup
2 tablespoons	= 1 liquid ounce
1 cup	= one-half pint
2 cups	= 1 pint
4 cups	= 1 quart
4 quarts	= 1 gallon

Equivalents…

1 pound sifted all-purpose flour	= 4 cups
1 pound white sugar	= 2 1/4-2 1/2 cups
1 pound brown sugar, firmly packed	= 2 1/8- 2 1/4 cups
1 lb. powdered sugar,	= 4 1/2 - 5 cups

sifted	
1 medium lemon rind, grated	= 1 tablespoon
1 medium lemon, juiced	= 3 tablespoons
1 medium orange, juiced	= one-quarter cup juice
4 ounces firm cheese (Cheddar, Jack, Swiss)	= 1 cup shredded, lightly packed
3 ounces hard cheese (Parmesan, Romano)	= one-half cup grated
4 ounce almonds or walnut meats	= 1 cup chopped
28 squares saltine (soda) crackers	= one-quarter cup crumbs
16 squares graham crackers	= 1 cup crumbs
24 two-inch vanilla wafers	= 1 cup crumbs
18 two-inch chocolate wafers	= 1 cup crumbs
1 package dry yeast	= 1 tablespoon

Metric Conversions...

To convert U.S. measurements to metric—or the other way around—get out the calculator!

ounces to grams:	multiply ounces by 28.3 for number of grams
grams to ounces:	multiply grams by .0353 for number of ounces
ounces to milliliters:	multiply ounces by 30 for number of milliliters
pounds to grams:	multiply pounds by 453.59 for number of grams
pounds to	multiply pounds by 0.45 for number of

kilograms:	kilograms
cups to liters:	multiply cups by 0.24 for number of liters
Fahrenheit to Celsius:	subtract 32 from the Fahrenheit degrees, multiply by 5, then divide by 9 to get degrees in Celsius
Celsius to Fahrenheit:	multiply Celsius degrees by 9, divide by 5, then add 32 to get degrees in Fahrenheit
inches to centimeters:	multiply inches by 2.54 for number of centimeters
centimeters to inches:	multiply centimeters by 0.39 to get number of inches

Food Substitutions...

Stuck without a needed ingredient? Here's a list of common substitutions. Your results may be a little different than usual, especially in baking.

Yogurt is truly a miracle-worker! Use it instead of...

• Mayonnaise	1 teaspoon Dijon mustard + 1 cup plain yogurt, salt and pepper
• Sour cream	Plain or vanilla yogurt + 1 teaspoon baking soda added to dry ingredients
• Cream cheese	Put plain yogurt in a coffee filter-lined strainer over a large bowl. Cover and refrigerate 24 hours. Save the whey for baking!
• Soup base	2 tablespoons flour + 1 cup plain yogurt

General Substitutions...

• 1 teaspoon Baking powder	One-third teaspoon baking soda + one-half teaspoon cream of tartar

• 1 cup cake flour	1 cup less 2 tablespoons all-purpose flour
• 1 tablespoon flour for thickening	1 1/2 teaspoons cornstarch or arrowroot
• 1 1/2 teaspoons arrowroot	1 tablespoon flour + 1 1/2 teaspoons cornstarch
• 1 cup self-rising flour	1 cup all-purpose flour plus 1 1/2 teaspoons baking powder and one-half teaspoon salt
• Whole eggs	2 egg whites for each whole egg + 1 tablespoon vegetable oil
• 1 cup sour cream	One-third cup melted butter + three-quarters cup buttermilk
• 1 cup buttermilk	1 cup milk mixed with 1 tablespoon white vinegar; let stand 10 minutes. Or 1 cup yogurt
• 1 oz. Baking chocolate	3 tablespoons cocoa + 1 tablespoon shortening or butter
• 1 cup dry bread crumbs	Three-quarters cup fine cracker crumbs

• 1 teaspoon lemon juice	One-half teaspoon white vinegar
• 1 clove garlic	One-eighth teaspoon garlic powder
• 1 tablespoons fresh herbs	1 teaspoon dried herbs
• 1 teaspoon Allspice	One-half teaspoon cinnamon and one-half teaspoon ground cloves
• 1 cup honey	1 1/4 cups sugar + one-quarter cup water
• 1 cup light corn syrup	1 1/4 cups light brown sugar and one-third cup water
• 1 cup dark corn syrup	Three-quarters cup light corn syrup plus one-quarter cup molasses OR 1 cup light corn syrup plus 1 tablespoon brown sugar

Kitchen Safety 101...

If there is one thing that every kitchen needs more than a good set of pots and pans or even a good sharp knife, it is a fire extinguisher. I can never stress it enough that when it comes to being a home chef, kitchen safety should always come first and foremost.

A lot of what I am about to tell you, you might already know. It is basic common sense, but we could all use a refresher course on kitchen safety every now and then. Here's why...

Did you know that on average, the kitchen sends over one million people to a hospital's emergency room every year? Not to mention the number of fires that start in a kitchen!

It is better to be safe than sorry, so, keep these tips in mind as you build on your career as a home chef....

- Always keep a domestic fire extinguisher in the kitchen.

- In the case of an actual fire, especially one that has spread to other areas in the kitchen, never try to fight it alone.

- Gather your family and leave immediately, and then, call 9-1-1 from a safe place.

- Always practice an exit strategy in the case of an emergency, even with small children.

- Do not position a fire extinguisher over the stove, as it would make the fire extinguisher inaccessible when you really need it.

- Be sure to train your entire family on how to use it.

- A compact fire blanket will suffocate flames from a deep fryer, which is often a major cause of house fires.

- Never throw water on a grease fire!

- Use cupboard locks so children can't get into harmful kitchen chemicals or other products.

- Buy detergents and other chemicals that have child proof lids or store them in high places.

- Never leave knives or scissors on counters.

- Store knives in a wood block.

- Always wash hands in warm soapy water before, after and before touching ready to eat food.

- If cuts or scrapes occur while cooking food, be sure to wash and cover the area immediately.

- Wipe hands on a separate kitchen towel, reserving the other dish towel that you dry dishes for dishes only.

- Bleach, disinfect or replace kitchen towels, cloths and sponges often, especially after working with raw foods.

- Return perishable foods, such as butter and milk to the refrigerator as soon as possible after use.

Now, if you are wondering why I said to return perishable items like butter and milk to the kitchen as soon as possible, then now is the time to talk about food safety...

The Truth About Food Safety...

Did you know that it is estimated that one in every six people could get sick from food poisoning this year alone?

Food poisoning not only sends more than 100,000 Americans to the hospital each year – it can also have severe long-term health consequences, or even death!

How you eat is truly how you live. Now is the time to really start thinking about eating better in order to live better. In this day and age, it often really easy to place the health of your friends, families and more importantly, yourself in other people hands based on the foods that we eat.

That is why the ability to conquer your kitchen becomes the key. The first step is maintaining the safety of the foods that you eat. That is why if you choose to forget about food safety in the foods that you eat at home or at a restaurant, you are setting yourself up for a recipe for disaster.

So before we get started, let's talk about some of myths, no, wait, let us call it what it is… outright lies that people continue to believe about the foods that we eat. Some of these lies might surprise, if not, shock you…

Lie number 1: Food poisoning isn't that big of a deal. You will just have to tough it out for a day or two, and then, it's all over.

The Truth: Many people don't know that food-borne illnesses can actually lead to severe long-term health conditions, such as kidney failure, chronic arthritis, and brain and nerve damage, and then, there is the estimated 3,000 Americans every year that die from food-borne illness.

Lie number 2: It's perfectly okay to thaw any meat on the counter. Since it starts out frozen, bacteria isn't really a problem.

The Truth: Actually, deadly bacteria grows more rapidly at room temperatures, so the counter is never a place you should thaw foods. Instead, try one of three ways to safely thaw out your next meal: allow it to thaw in the fridge, pop it in the microwave and use the defrost feature or allow it to thaw in cold water. Yes, cold water! Hot water only increases the ability for this deadly bacteria to reproduce.

Lie number 3: When cleaning your kitchen, the more bleach you use the better. More bleach kills more bacteria, so it's safer for my family.

The Truth: The truth is more of anything isn't always the best thing. I will simply use one tablespoon of liquid, unscented bleach for every one quart of water that I am using to clean with.

Lie number 4: You don't need to wash fruits or vegetables if you are just going to peel them.

The Truth: Not washing your fruit makes it easier to transfer bacteria from the peel or rind you're cutting to the inside of your fruits and veggies. You should wash any fruit or vegetable, even if you plan to peel it.

Stop and think about where your produce came from—the ground. Second, it is often bathed in pesticides to keep it from being devoured by insects and bugs before it hits your table. My suggestion, wash it thoroughly!

For me, I soak my veggies and fruits in vinegar and water for about two to three minutes, and then, rinse it for about thirty seconds in a colander under the tap.

You will be shocked at how murky your vinegar-water soaking solution looks after this process. That murkiness is what you could have been putting in your body!

Lie number 5: To get rid of any bacteria on any meat, poultry, or seafood, I should rinse off the juices with water first.

The Truth: When you rinse meat, poultry, or seafood with water, this can actually increase your chances of food poisoning by splashing juices (and any bacteria they might contain) onto your sink and counter tops.

The only way you can ensure the safety of your meat, poultry and seafood is to make sure that you cook it at the proper temperature.

Lie number 6: The only reason why you should let any food sit after it's been microwaved is to make sure you don't burn yourself on food that's too hot.

The Truth: When you let food "sit," this is called "standing time." It helps your food cook more completely by allowing the colder areas of your food to absorb the heat from hotter areas of the food.

Lie number 7: Your leftovers are safe to eat until they smell bad.

The Truth: Did you know that some kinds of bacteria that cause food poisoning do not affect the look, smell, or taste of food. That is why I have included a list of storage times in this book to ensure that you will know when it is time to throw that food out.

Lie number 8: Once food has been cooked, all the bacteria have been killed, so I don't need to worry once it's "done."

The Truth: Actually, the possibility of bacterial growth actually increases after cooking, because the drop in temperature allows bacteria to thrive. This is why keeping cooked food warmed to the right temperature is critical for food safety.

Lie number 9: Marinades are acidic, which is supposed to kill bacteria, so it's okay to marinate foods on the counter.

The Truth: Even in the presence of acidic marinade, bacteria can grow very rapidly at room temperatures. To marinate foods safely, it's important to marinate them in the refrigerator until you are ready to cook it.

Lie number 10: If I really want my produce to be safe, I should wash fruits and veggies with soap or detergent before I use them.

The Truth: Never use soaps or detergents on produce, since these products can linger on foods and are not safe for consumption. Using clean running water is actually the best way to remove bacteria and wash produce safely.

Now that you know the truth, for the first time in any cookbook that I have seen in a long time, let me show you how to keep the foods that you eat stored safely...

Food Storage 101...

As you already know, some foods are more frequently associated with food poisoning or food-borne illness than others. That is why it is always important to remember these four simple steps for cleaning, separating, cooking and chilling food in your kitchen....:

Clean...

- Wash your hands with warm, soapy water for at least 20 seconds before preparing food.

- Wash counter surfaces, utensils, dishes and cutting boards with hot, soapy water before preparing food.

- Remember that paper towels work well for cleaning any surfaces.

- Cloth towels can spread bacteria and should be washed frequently.

Separate...

- Keep raw meat, poultry and seafood away from other foods while shopping and in the refrigerator. The juices could drip and spread bacteria.

- Use different cutting boards when preparing food, one for raw meat and one for ready-to-eat foods.

- Don't allow cooked or ready-to-eat foods to come in contact with raw meats.

Cook...

- Use a thermometer to measure the internal temperature of cooked foods to make sure that they reach a safe temperature.

- If using a microwave oven, take some food safety precautions not to get burned, like using microwave-safe containers.

- For even microwave cooking, cover the food, rotate and stir the contents to prevent hot and cold spots.

- Allow microwave-cooked food to stand about two minutes before serving.

Chill...

- Refrigerate foods within two hours of preparation.

- Do not defrost foods at room temperature.

- Foods should be thawed in the refrigerator, under cold running water, as part of cooking or in the microwave.

- Microwave-thawed food should be cooked immediately.

- To chill foods quickly, store leftovers in shallow containers.

- Cool air must always circulate in the refrigerator.

- Do not pack your refrigerator too full and be sure to monitor the temperature with a refrigerator thermometer.

According to the United States Department of Health and Human Services, here is more suggested ways to protect you and your family from further food borne illnesses for the following categories of food...

Raw Meat:

Raw meat may contain bacteria, such as E. coli, salmonella, and listeria, or parasites. Thorough cooking destroys these harmful organisms, but meat can become contaminated again if it is not handled and stored properly.

Turkey

Turkey is often associated with holidays and parties. But, turkey can also be associated with food-borne illness if it is not thawed, prepared, cooked, and stored properly.

Chicken and Other Poultry

Poultry may contain such harmful and deadly forms of bacteria such as salmonella, listeria and campylobacter. Washing chicken and other poultry does not remove bacteria. You can kill these bacteria only by cooking chicken to the proper temperature.

Seafood

Like raw meat, raw seafood may contain bacteria that can be destroyed only by cooking. Some seafood may also contain toxins, such as mercury, which may be harmful for young children or an unborn baby.

Eggs and Egg Products

Fresh eggs must be handled carefully. Even eggs with clean, uncracked shells may occasionally contain salmonella. To prevent food poisoning, keep eggs refrigerated, cook eggs until yolks are firm, and cook foods containing eggs thoroughly.

Milk, Cheese, and Dairy Products

Raw milk, as well as cheeses made with raw milk, may contain E. coli, salmonella, and listeria. That's why it's important to make sure that milk has been pasteurized, which kills harmful bacteria.

Fresh Fruits, Vegetables, and Juices

Fresh produce may come in contact with harmful bacteria from many sources, from contaminated soil and water in the fields to a contaminated cutting board in the kitchen. Fruit and vegetable juices must be treated to kill bacteria.

Nuts, Grains, and Beans

Nuts, grains, beans, and other legumes, and their by-products, are found in a wide variety of foods. Since these foods are ingredients in so many food products, contamination or mislabeling of allergens can pose a widespread risk.

How To Read Food Label Dates...

Here's another question for you... Do you know what the dates on many canned and boxed goods mean? You should it could be costing you thousands of dollars in wasted food.

Start saving money right now by making a date with your fridge! Just by opening the fridge door and checking the 'use by' dates on what's inside, you can begin saving money.

How often do you find that the 'use by' date on a gallon of milk or a package of ground turkey or chicken has come and gone and you end up throwing it away? That is money that you are wasting!

Meat, fish and ready meals are often the most expensive things we buy, so it helps to get into the habit of regularly checking the dates on perishable items in your fridge. When in doubt, move them into the freezer, if you don't think you'll have time to eat them or cook them for tonight's supper.

When you get home with your meats, it is always a good idea to transfer as much as you can straight into the freezer. If you have large packets of chicken pieces or fish, divide them up, clean, season and freeze individual portions. You can even use a permanent marker to write in very large writing the "use by" or expiration date right on the package.

So What About The Dates On Certain Food Labels...

Many foods have a date stamped on the label. These dates can help you choose foods that are fresh and safe to eat. You will see different dates on different types of foods.

The **"Pull-By" or "Sell-By..."** date is used on foods like milk, cheese, and packaged meats. It is the last date the product should be sold. These foods are usually stored in the refrigerator. They will stay fresh and safe for few days after this date if you store them properly.

"Freshness" or "Best-If-Used-By" dates are used on products like bakery goods or packaged cereals. The date is the last day the product can keep its best quality. After this date, the food may lose some of its freshness and nutritional value.

An **"Expiration" or "Use-By"** date is the last date the food should be eaten or used. It is used mostly on products such as refrigerated dough and yeast.

A **"Pack"** date is the date the food was manufactured or processed and packaged. This type of date is used for foods that can be kept for a long time, like canned goods.

With these dates in mind, you can save thousands of dollars in wasted groceries and and even more time having to throw away foods that will go bad too quickly.

Now, I think it about time that we talk about the foods without a date...

Refrigerator And Freezer Storage Times...

These short, but safe time limits for home-refrigerated foods will keep them from spoiling or becoming dangerous to eat. The guidelines for freezer storage are for quality only. Some freezable foods remain safe indefinitely.

Category	Food	Refrigerator (40 °F or below)	Freezer (0 °F or below)
Salads	Egg, chicken, ham, tuna & macaroni salads	3 to 5 days	Does not freeze well
Hot dogs	opened package	1 week	1 to 2 months
	unopened package	2 weeks	1 to 2 months
Luncheon meat	opened package or deli sliced	3 to 5 days	1 to 2 months
	unopened package	2 weeks	1 to 2 months
Bacon &	Bacon	7 days	1 month

Sausage	Sausage, raw chicken, turkey, pork, beef	1 to 2 days	1 to 2 months
Hamburger & Other Ground Meats	Hamburger, ground beef, turkey, veal, pork, lamb, & mixtures of them	1 to 2 days	3 to 4 months
Fresh Beef, Veal, Lamb & Pork	Steaks	3 to 5 days	6 to 12 months
	Chops	3 to 5 days	4 to 6 months
	Roasts	3 to 5 days	4 to 12 months
Fresh Poultry	Chicken or turkey, whole	1 to 2 days	1 year
	Chicken or turkey, pieces	1 to 2 days	9 months
Soups & Stews	Vegetable or meat added	3 to 4 days	2 to 3 months
Leftovers	Cooked meat or	3 to 4 days	2 to 6

	poultry		months
	Chicken nuggets or patties	3 to 4 days	1 to 3 months
	Pizza	3 to 4 days	1 to 2 months

Egg Storage Chart...

For storage times for eggs and foods made with eggs. Always label food with the content and the date it was made and refer to this chart for when it expires...

Product	Refrigerator	Freezer
Raw eggs in shell	3 to 5 weeks	Do not freeze. Instead, beat yolks and whites together; then freeze.
Raw egg whites	2 to 4 days	12 months
Raw egg yolks	2 to 4 days	Yolks do not freeze well.
Raw egg, accidentally frozen in shell	Use immediately after thawing.	Keep frozen; then refrigerate to thaw.
Hard-cooked eggs	1 week	Do not freeze.
Egg substitutes, liquid, Unopened	10 days	12 months
Egg substitutes, liquid, Opened	3 days	Do not freeze.

Egg substitutes, frozen, Unopened	After thawing, 7 days or refer to "Use-By" date.	12 months
Egg substitutes, frozen, Opened	After thawing, 3 days or refer to "Use-By" date.	Do not freeze.
Casseroles with eggs	3 to 4 days	After baking, 2 to 3 months.
Eggnog Commercial	3 to 5 days	6 months
Eggnog Homemade	2 to 4 days	Do not freeze.
Pies Pumpkin or pecan	3 to 4 days	After baking, 1 to 2 months.
Pies Custard and chiffon	3 to 4 days	Do not freeze.
Quiche with filling	3 to 4 days	After baking, 1 to 2 months.

Food Thermometers...

Why is using a food thermometer important?

- Cooking by color can be misleading. One in every four hamburgers turns brown before it has reached a safe internal temperature.
  - Using a food thermometer can prevent overcooking.
  - Public health data since 2000 show that our food has more than five times the number of dangerous bacteria.
  - You can become sick from 20 minutes to six weeks after eating food with some types of harmful bacteria.
  - Young children, pregnant women, people over age 65 and people with chronic illnesses are at a higher risk for food-borne illness.
- Getting sick from a food-borne illness can cause serious health problems, even death.
- The only sure way to know if your food is done is to use a food thermometer.

How do you use a food thermometer?

- When measuring the temperature of a roast or chicken, insert the food thermometer in the thickest part away from bones.
- To measure the temperature of soups, stews and casseroles, insert the food thermometer in the center away from the bottom.
- Some thermometers can be left in the meat during the cooking process. Before using a thermometer in this way, be sure your thermometer is oven-safe!

Safe Minimum Cooking Temperatures...

Use this chart and a food thermometer to ensure that meat, poultry, seafood, and other cooked foods reach a safe minimum internal temperature.

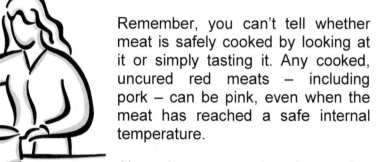

Remember, you can't tell whether meat is safely cooked by looking at it or simply tasting it. Any cooked, uncured red meats – including pork – can be pink, even when the meat has reached a safe internal temperature.

Also, always remember that resting time or the time that any food is left standing. After you remove meat from a grill, oven, or other heat source, allow it to rest for the specified amount of time. During the rest time, its temperature remains constant or continues to rise, which destroys harmful bacteria.

Category:	**Food:**	**Temperature (°F):**	**Rest Time:**
Ground Meat & Meat Mixtures	Beef, Pork, Veal, Lamb	160°F	None
	Turkey, Chicken	165°F	None
Fresh Beef, Veal, Lamb	Steaks, roasts, chops	145°F	3 minutes
Poultry	Chicken & Turkey, whole	165°F	None
	Poultry	165°F	None

	breasts, roasts		
	Poultry thighs, legs, wings	165°F	None
	Duck & Goose	165°F	None
	Stuffing (cooked alone or in bird)	165°F	None
Pork and Ham	Fresh pork	145°F	3 minutes
	Fresh ham (raw)	145°F	3 minutes
	Precooked ham (to reheat)	140°F	None
Eggs & Egg Dishes	Eggs	Cook until yolk and white are firm	None
	Egg dishes	160°F	None
Leftovers & Casseroles	Leftovers	165°F	None
	Casseroles	165°F	None
Seafood	Fin Fish	145°F or cook until flesh is opaque and separates easily with a fork.	None
	Shrimp, lobster, and crabs	Cook until flesh is pearly and opaque.	None
	Clams, oysters, and mussels	Cook until shells open during cooking.	None
	Scallops	Cook until flesh is milky white or opaque and firm.	None

Roasting 101...

Always season your meats well for up to 24 hours before you decide to begin roasting. This allows the flavors that you will later savor to take hold.

Then, use the recommended cooking times and temperatures guidelines to ensure that the meat is cooked to the minimum safe internal temperature.

An accurate meat thermometer helps avoiding food-borne illness that can be caused by under cooked food.

Cut of Meat	Weight (pounds)	Oven Temperature	Cooking Time (minutes/pounds)
Beef Rib Roast	4 to 6	325°F	26 to 30 (rare) 34 to 38 (medium)
	6 to 8	325°F	23 to 25 (rare) 27 to 30 (medium)
	8 to 10	325°F	19 to 21 (rare) 23 to 25 (medium)
Beef Tenderloin, whole	4 to 6	425°F	45 to 60 minutes total
Beef Top Round Roast	2-1/2 to 4	325°F	25 to 30 (rare) 30 to 35 (medium)
	4 to 6	325°F	20 to 25 (rare) 25 to 30 (medium)
Veal Loin Roast, boneless	2 to 3	300°F to 325°F	18 to 20 (medium) 22 to 24 (well)
Veal Rump Roast,	2 to 3	300°F to 325°F	33 to 35 (medium) 37 to 40 (well)

boneless			
Veal Shoulder Roast, boneless	2-1/2 to 3	300°F to 325°F	31 to 34 (medium) 34 to 37 (well)
Lamb Leg, bone-in	7 to 9	325°F	15 to 20 (rare) 20 to 25 (medium) 25 to 30 (well)
Lamb Rib Roast	2 to 3	375°F	25 to 30 (rare) 30 to 35 (medium) 35 to 40 (well)
Pork Tenderloin	1/2 to 1	425°F	27 to 29
Pork Loin Top Loin Roast (double, boneless)	3 to 4	325°F	29 to 34
Pork Loin Top Loin Roast (boneless)	2 to 4	325°F	23 to 33
Pork Crown Roast	6 to 10	325°F	20 to 25
Pork Leg or Fresh Ham (whole, bone-in)	12	325°F	23 to 25
Fully-Cooked Boneless Ham (with 1/2 cup water, covered)	1-1/2 to 2	325°F	29 to 33
	3 to 4	325°F	19 to 23
	6 to 8	325°F	16 to 20
	9 to 11	325°F	12 to 16

Slow Cooking 101...

The beauty of using a crock pot, or slow cooker, is that it's really simple. Prep your ingredients, add them to the slow cooker and press "Start."

The crock pot, or slow cooker, is one of the best time saving appliances in the kitchen. It's great for beginning cooks because all you have to do is fill it and turn it on.

Hours later, you will have a house filled with wonderful smells and dinner ready for the table. But, first, let's make sure that you have what you need to do it right.

With my help, let's turn that good slow-cooked meal into a great one...

Purchasing and Safety...

- When purchasing a crock pot, look for one with a removable liner, especially one that is dishwasher safe. They are much easier to clean.

- If you have a non-removable liner, however, all is not lost! Line your crock pot with a cooking bag and you'll have no cleanup at all. Spray the inside of the liner with cooking spray before you fill it to make cleanup even easier.

- Always keep the area around your crock pot clear. Free of clutter and free of any children or anybody who can trip over the cord.

- It's safe to walk away and leave your slow cooker unattended while it does its job, but a few precautions never hurt.

- The sides generate some moderate heat, so always position the cooker six inches or so away from any walls or other appliances so the heat can dissipate.

- The bottom is made to be safe on any counter, but you can set it on a cooling rack if you're concerned.

- Always ensure that all food reaches 140 degrees Fahrenheit. That is the temperature that the food needs to reach as quickly as possible.

- Always test the food temperature after four hours of cooking on the lowest setting. That temperature should be at least 140 degrees. If it isn't, there's a problem with your crock pot and you should get a new one right away.

- For food safety reasons, it's a good idea to cook on the highest setting for the first hour to quickly bring the temperature up to 140 degrees. Then, turn the dial to the lowest setting and allow your food to finish cooking.

- The lowest setting should be about 200 degrees, and the highest setting should be about 300 degrees. (Please note that both of these temps are well above the minimum safe temperature of 140 degrees.)

- Never put frozen foods in the crock pot. All foods should be defrosted before cooking so that the food's temperature can reach 140 degrees as quickly as possible.

- A good many slow-cooker recipes require only some basic prep work like cutting vegetables or trimming meat before everything gets dumped into the slow cooker. If you have time, you'll get better flavor in your final dish if you also brown the meat and sear the vegetables.

- Always remember that one hour on HIGH is equal to two hours on LOW.

- Always remove cooked food from the crock pot or liner before you refrigerate the cooked food.

- Remember that because the liner is made of such thick material, the food won't cool down quickly enough to prevent the growth of harmful bacteria.

Crock Pot (Slow Cooker) General Cooking Tips...

- The setting that you choose merely dictates how quickly the slow cooker gets to that temperature. The lower settings (usually 8 hour and 10 hour cooking times) will heat food gently, whereas the higher settings (4 hour and 6 hour cooking times) will heat it more quickly.

- Modern slow cookers are designed to bring food to temperature within a safe window of time and hold it there.

- Only fill the crock pot one half to two thirds full. The foods will not cook properly if the appliance is filled to the brim. If the food and liquid level is lower, the foods will cook too quickly.

- If your recipe uses liquid, it should come about halfway up the ingredients (or less). Very little liquid will evaporate during cooking, so you generally don't need more than the recommended amount of it!

- Foods cooked on the bottom of the slow cooker will cook faster and will be moister because they are immersed in the simmering liquid.

- Always remove skin from poultry and trim excess fat from meats. These fats will melt with long cooking times, and will add an unpleasant texture to the finished dish. Fatty foods will also cook too quickly.

- You can thicken the juices and concentrate flavors by removing the lid and cooking on HIGH for the last half hour of cooking time.

- Most meats require eight hours of cooking on the lowest setting. Cheaper cuts of meat work better in the slow cooker. Cheaper cuts of meat have less fat, which makes them more suited to crock pot cooking.

- Moist, long cooking times result in very tender meats, saving you time and money.

- Follow the layering instructions carefully. Vegetables do not cook as quickly as meat, so they should be placed in the bottom of the appliance.

- The lid should fit snugly over the slow cooker with no gaps for steam to escape. Slow cookers depend on bringing your food up to a stable temperature (usually around 210°) and keeping it there.

- If the lid isn't snug, the cooker won't work as efficiently. If your lid has been dropped on the floor one too many times and has some gaps, wrap a sheet of aluminum foil over the top of the cooker to seal everything in.

- Don't lift the lid to stir, especially if you are cooking on the low setting. Each time you lift the lid, enough heat will escape that the cooking time should be extended by 20 minutes to half an hour.

- To check progress without lifting the lid, turn the cover until the condensation falls off. Then, it becomes easier to see inside.

Specific Crock Pot (Slow Cooker) Cooking Tips...

- Ground meats should be cooked in a skillet before cooking in the crock pot.

- Seafood should be added during the last hour of cooking time, or it will overcook and the seafood, especially shrimp, will have a rubbery texture to it.

- Large pieces of meat can be browned before cooking in the crock pot, but this step isn't necessary. This type of browning, though, will add color and helps in flavor development in your food.

- Cayenne pepper and hot sauce tend to become bitter if cooked for long periods of time. Use small amounts and add toward the end of the cooking time.

- Add tender vegetables like tomatoes, mushrooms and zucchini during the last 45 minutes of cooking time so that they don't overcook.

- Dairy products should be added during the last 30 minutes of cooking time, unless the recipes states otherwise.

- Liquids do not boil away in the crock pot, so if you are making a recipe that wasn't specifically developed for the crock pot, reduce the liquid by 1/3 to 1/2 of the recommended amount, unless you are cooking rice or making soup.

- Stir in spices for the last hour of cooking. They will lose flavor if cooked with the rest of the ingredients for the long cooking period.

- Like any other dish, slow cooker dishes need to be eaten, cooled, and stored within a safe time period, so make sure you're around when the cooking cycle ends.

- Most modern models will automatically switch over to a "warming" cycle at the end of cooking if you're not right there. This should keep food hot enough to prevent it from spoiling, but it can overcook your food if used for too long.

Determining Slow Cooking Times...

You should know that most slow cooker recipes average 6 to 10 hours of cook time. If you want to convert your favorite recipes to the slow cooker, use the following guidelines.

Ideally, you want to choose recipes where most, if not all, of the ingredients can be added at the beginning, leaving you free to do other things. For the following meats, after properly cleaning and seasoning, they can be added to your crock pot or slow cooker as the basis for your entire meal.

Meat Cut	Meat Weight	Low Cook Time	High Cook Time
Large Pork Roast*	6-7 lbs	9 ½ hours	7 ½ hours
Pork Loin	3-4 lbs	6 hours	5 hours
Poultry**	6 lbs	7 ½ hours	6 ¼ hours
Beef Roast	3-4 lbs	8 hours	5 ¾ hours
Stew Meat	3 lbs	6 hours	4 ¾ hours
Fish***	2 lbs	3 ½ hours	1 ½ hours

* Pork butt, pork shoulder
** Whole chicken, Bone-in turkey breast
*** If fish is stirred in after slow cooker has been fully heated to stabilization/simmer point, it will cook within 15-30 minutes.

Note: All cooking times are approximate. Appropriate cooking time varies according to specific meat characteristics, like fat content and connective tissue, as well as other ingredients added to dish, including liquid, size of meat cubes, type of vegetable, size of vegetable dice, how high slow cooker is filled, etc.

You can always check to make sure your food has safely finished cooking by using a meat or instant-read thermometer.

Insert the thermometer into the thickest part of the cooked food without touching bone or the cooking container to get an accurate reading. With all of this in mind, you will go from preparing a good meal to a great one.

Since I did mention vegetables and how quickly they cook in a crock pot, let's talk about keeping them fresh...

Storing And Keeping Fresh Vegetables...

So okay, listen, when it comes to meats, sure you can pop  those meats into a freezer and everything is okay, but what about fresh fruits and vegetables? I love fresh fruits and vegetables. But, I honestly don't have time to go to a produce stand or a farmer's market every day to pick up some fresh fruits and vegetables for what I want to make.

Like I said before, every bit of food that you should buy should have a purpose. Especially when it is estimated that every year almost 500 pounds of food is tossed out by families and people like me and you, according to the United States Department of Agriculture, with one fourth of that food being fresh fruit and vegetables.

The same vegetables that could have provided a good source of vitamins and vegetables that you and/or your family needs will wind up in the trash. Why? They simply didn't come with a label to tell you when to use them.

You should know that there is a way that you can save yourself time and money and stop your fruits and vegetables from going bad quickly. Let me explain...

When I am in the market, I have a very bad habit. I tend to buy my vegetables last. I try to avoid the center of the store, because that is where the processed foods are. I stick to the dairy, vegetables and the meat sections, but my vegetables are always bought last. I treat it like I treat my ice cream, I want them to stay cool.

When I get home, I try to get my food put away as quickly as possible. It helps to bag like items together. The problem is keeping them fresh once I get home. Here's what you should do...

The first thing that I do is never mix my fruits and vegetables together. That is right, I keep my onions with my onions and my peppers with my peppers. Many of your fruits may be releasing high levels of ethylene gas, an odorless, colorless gas, which helps ripen certain fruits and vegetables, and it is speeding up the decay of certain fruits and vegetables that are very sensitive promoting their decay.

Second, I go through my fruits and vegetables to check for any piece that might be starting to go bad. One bad apple can really spoil a whole bunch and it can create a domino effect when it comes to the other fruits and vegetables around it. When one goes bad, the mold and bacteria spreads to other pieces of fruit causing their demise.

Third, when storing certain fruits and vegetables, I am always aware of where I can store some things. Some vegetables should never go in the refrigerators. Store them where they belong, in a bowl on the counter or your table. (My mother had a hanging fruit basket.) If you don't, they tend to lose their flavor and moisture and they start to go bad. Once they are fully ripe though, you can put them in the refrigerator, which can help them last slightly longer.

Fourth, always let your fruits and vegetables breath. Never seal them in an airtight bag or plastic, this will only speed up the process that will cause them to go bad. Fruits and vegetables need to breath.

Lastly, when it comes to potatoes, onions, winter squash, or, garlic, always store them in a cool, dark, dry cabinet, and they can last up to a month or more. But, always be sure to separate them so that their flavors and smells don't migrate. You don't want your potatoes smelling like onions.

So, with that in mind, here's how to store certain vegetables...

Always refrigerate these fruits and vegetables:

- Apples
- Apricots
- Cantaloupe
- Figs
- Honeydew

Don't refrigerate these fruits and vegetables:

- Avocados
- Bananas, unripe
- Nectarines
- Peaches
- Pears
- Plums
- Tomatoes

Keep these seperated:

- Bananas, ripe
- Broccoli
- Brussels sprouts
- Cabbage
- Carrots
- Cauliflower
- Cucumbers
- Eggplant
- Lettuce and other leafy greens
- Parsley
- Peas
- Peppers
- Squash
- Sweet potatoes
- Watermelon

Remember what I said about fresh fruits and vegetables not coming with an expiration label. Here is a helpful cheat sheet on just how long some fruits and vegetables will last in your refrigerator or on your counter.

These fresh fruits and vegetables will last about one to three days...

- Artichokes
- Asparagus
- Avocados
- Bananas
- Basil

- Broccoli
- Cherries
- Corn
- Dill
- Green beans

- Mushrooms
- Mustard greens
- Strawberries
- Watercress

These fresh fruits and vegetables will last about four to six days...

- Arugula
- Cucumbers
- Eggplant

- Grapes
- Lettuce
- Lime

- Mesclun
- Pineapple
- Zucchini

These fresh fruits and vegetables will last about four to six days...

- Apricots
- Bell peppers
- Blueberries
- Brussels sprouts
- Cauliflower
- Grapefruit

- Leeks
- Lemons
- Mint
- Oranges
- Oregano
- Parsley

- Peaches
- Pears
- Plums
- Spinach
- Tomatoes
- Watermelon

These fresh fruits and vegetables will last over seven days...

- Apples
- Beets
- Cabbage

- Carrots
- Celery
- Garlic

- Onions
- Potatoes
- Winter squash

Veggie Cooking Times...

If you are like millions of people, you have fallen into a habit when it comes to your choice of vegetables... corn, peas  and broccoli. The new dinner plate calls for two servings of vegetables and you might want to try something new, but don't know how long to cook it.

Even, if you're new to the kitchen, or just trying to shake things up a little, it's helpful to know which vegetables cook in a similar manner. I can help you with that.

Right now, it also doesn't matter if you're trying out a new fresh vegetable, go ahead and buy up a big bag at the farmers' market and try cooking it a few different ways until you find the one best for you.

Of course, you can use a wide variety of cooking methods (steamed, grilled, roasted, sautéed) and the size of the vegetable will further determine the cooking time.

You can also rely on the cooking time on the packaging, if you are going the canned or frozen vegetable route. I always add a little butter and sugar to my peas and corn to help bring out their natural sweetness.

When it comes to fresh vegetables, you should always cook vegetables until soft, but so that they still have a bite to them (think green beans that remain firm rather than droopy).

Personal tastes may vary as to how you like your vegetables, but the following cooking times should suffice to start with, and can be varied slightly the next time that you cook them.

To keep vegetables from overcooking before serving, submerge them in ice water to stop from cooking, and again , reheat them briefly in boiling water when you're ready to serve. Season them to your taste, and then, enjoy!

The following is a general cooking time cheat sheet (in minutes) and the cooking times may vary slightly depending on the quality and freshness of the vegetable, if you intend to boil, bake, steam or saute them.

Cooks Quickly (5 minutes or less)

• Asparagus
• Broccoli
• Carrots
• Corn
• Eggplant
• Green Beans
• Mushrooms
• Peas
• Spinach

Cooks in 10 to 15 minutes

• Brussels Sprouts
• Cauliflower
• Squash
• Cabbage

Just Keep Cooking (15 minutes and beyond)

• Artichokes
• Beets
• Collard Greens and other hearty greens
• Potatoes

Perfect Pasta 101...

Contrary to popular belief, cooking pasta is not as easy as boiling water, but in order for you to cook it correctly, you have to pay attention to the details.

You can ensure that you are serving your friends, your family and yourself the best dishes ever by simply following these simple steps…

For every one pound of pasta, bring 5 quarts of cold water to a rolling boil. More water than pasta keeps the pasta from turning out mushy, sticky or clumping.

Don't become tempted to place the pasta in the water before it comes to a boil. You will know that it has come to a boil when you see the big air bubbles begin to rise and burst.

Always use cold water to start to cook anything. It might be tempting to use hot water, but it doesn't make that much of a difference.

It is a common misconception that salt will make your pasta boil faster, the truth is you would need a lot of salt to make that happen.

Salting your water should only be used to enhance the flavor of the pasta; because otherwise people will overdo it and you pasta will have a salty after taste.

Only add a tablespoon of salt to your water if you do, it allows the pasta to absorb the salty flavor. If you try to add salt afterwards, it will lose that ability to accent the flavor of the food.

Remember excessive salt robs the body of water and forces you to drink something to hydrate yourself, usually the wrong kind of drinks, like soda or juices. This leads to unnecessary water weight gain and weight from those unnecessary calories. So always limit how much salt that you use.

Always remember to only add pasta to your boiling water once you see the big bubbles start to form that lets you know that your water is boiling.

Never add any olive oil, margarine or butter to your water. This will cause your pasta to be oily preventing the sauce from sticking to it later and adding the intended flavor.

Stir to keep the pasta from sticking within the first two minutes of cooking the pasta. This is the point before the starch is released into the water.

Place the lid back on the pot to help bring the water back to a boil. This is an important step because if you don't, the pasta will be sitting in hot water, resulting in mushy pasta.

Once the pot is boiling again, remove the lid for the remaining cook time to prevent the pasta from boiling over.

You can also lay a long wooden spoon across the top of the pot. The wooden spoon breaks the bubbles up and prevents the water from boiling over.

Follow the package directions for cook times. As a general guideline: perfectly cooked pasta that is "al dente," or firm to the bite, yet cooked through. This practice requires you to test it yourself when the time is close.

If it is under cooked, it will have a stiff and chalky core.

If it is overcooked, your noodles will be limp and mushy.

Remember that once you decide that the pasta is done, it will take you several seconds to turn off the burner, lift the pot and pour the contents into the colander.

During this time, the pasta continues to cook, so begin testing for doneness 2-3 minutes before the end of the suggested cooking time.

Once your pasta is ready, turn off the heat and scoop out 1 cup of pasta cooking water. That soupy looking water you used to throw down the drain is actually a miracle ingredient!

Save this pasta water, because it contains essential starch that can be used later to adjust the consistency of your sauce, from thickening it to thinning it, if you need it.

Quickly drain the pasta into a colander in the sink.

Do no rinse the pasta. The starch from the pasta helps your sauce adhere to your pasta, but rinsing will cool the pasta and prevent absorption of your sauce and its flavor.

The only time you should ever rinse your pasta is when you are going to use it in a cold dish like a pasta salad. In cases such as those, rinsing the pasta helps to stop the cooking process.

Next, toss pasta in a warmed saucepan with your prepared sauce. You don't want to drain the pasta well. You want your pasta to be loosely drained, still retaining some pasta water. Cook together for about 2 minutes, and then, enjoy!

Pasta Cooking Times...

Pasta is one of the simplest and quickest meals that you can ever make. I have listed different pastas that you can whip

up in minutes and simply add a cooked meat like chicken or shrimp and a sauce to and you will have a delicious meal.

Remember that all pasta cooking times may vary one to two minutes. Test doneness at the shortest time.

Dry Pasta Cooking Times			
	Cooking Time (minutes)		Cooking Time (minutes)
Acini de pepe	5 to 6	**Penne**	9 to 13
Capellini	5 to 6	**Radiatore**	9 to 11
Egg noodles, regular	8 to 10	**Rigatoni**	12 to 15
Egg noodles, extra wide	10 to 12	**Rosa marina** (orzo)	8 to 10

Elbow macaroni	8 to 10	Rotelle	10 to 12
Farfalle	13 to 15	Rotini	8 to 10
Fettuccine	11 to 13	Shells, jumbo	12 to 15
Fusilli	11 to 13	Shells, medium and small	9 to 11
Japanese curly noodles	4 to 5	Soba noodles	6 to 7
Lasagna noodles	12 to 15	Spaghetti	8 to 10
Linguine	9 to 13	Vermicelli	5 to 7
Mafalda	8 to 10	Wagon wheel	10 to 12
Manicotti	10 to 12	Ziti	14 to 15
Refrigerated or Fresh Pasta			
	Cooking Time		Cooking Time

	(minutes)		(minutes)
Capellini	1 to 2	**Linguine**	1 to 2
Farfalle	2 to 3	**Ravioli**	6 to 8
Fettuccine	1 to 2	**Tortellini**	8 to 10
Lasagna	2 to 3		

Pasta Yield Charts

Type of Pasta	Uncooked	Cooked	Servings
Short Pastas Penne, Rotini, Shells, Wagon Wheels	6 to 7 oz.	4 cups	4 to 6
Long Pastas Capellini, Linguine, Spaghetti, Vermicelli	7 to 8 oz.	4 cups	4 to 6
Egg Noodles	8 oz.	4 to 5 cups	4 to 6 Cups

Baking 101...

You already know that every ingredient has a purpose when it comes to baking. It is either there to for stabilizing, sweetening, leavening, thickening, flavoring or more.

Even then, there are certain things that you need to do in order to make your baking attempts a success. Let's start with the basics:

Basic Flour Information...

All-Purpose Flour...

- All-purpose flour is the most well-known and used flour. There is no leavening agent added (unlike self-rising flour) and it has a moderate protein content.

- The reason protein content is important when determining what kind of flour to use in relation to texture is because the protein creates gluten when mixed or kneaded in the dough.

- The higher the gluten content the more chewy texture there will be to the baked good.

Bread Flour...

- Bread flour has the highest protein content of any of the flour.

- Bread flour is used here to create more chew due to more gluten.

- You can substitute bread flour for all-purpose flour cup for cup.
- Just remember the texture will be chewier than with all-purpose flour.

Cake Flour...

- Cake flour has the lowest protein content which is why it is most commonly used in cakes.
- Cake flour produces the tender crumbs that we desire in cakes.
- Because of the low protein content, cake flour also weighs less than all-purpose flour.
- When substituting cake flour for all-purpose flour, add 2 tablespoons more per cup.

Self-Rising Flour...

- Self-rising flour is nothing more than all-purpose flour with baking powder and salt already mixed in.
- Remember that one cup of self-rising flour has about one teaspoon baking powder and 1/2 teaspoon salt already mixed in.
- With this knowledge you can make adjustments as needed. You can also use this knowledge to make your own self-rising flour if a recipe calls for it and you only have all-purpose.

Whole Wheat Flour...

- Whole wheat flour is flour that still has the bran and germ in it, as opposed the white flour that has been refined and the bran and germ removed. These parts of the flour have more nutrients which is why a lot of people prefer to use them over white flour.

- In baking, if you want to substitute whole wheat flour for all-purpose, subtract 2 tablespoons per cup.

- Whole wheat flour has a more rough texture than that of soft, white flour due the bran. This is why a lot of people do not prefer it.

- Use half white flour and half whole wheat when you want to up the nutritious factor instead of all whole wheat because of the texture.

- Also, notice that cookies with at least some whole wheat flour in them do not get as flat as those with only white flour.

- Use half whole wheat flour to also get a taller cookie.

Using Substitutions…

While it is always best to use the ingredient called for in a recipe, occasional emergency substitutions must be made. The substitutions below will work, but, in some cases, the flavor and/or texture will be different. Like if you run out of eggs, use a half of a banana for every egg. I use apple sauce instead of oil in some recipes for better cakes and cookies. It is always your choice to do so.

The Truth About Gluten-Free…

- Gluten is most commonly known for causing some severe wheat-related allergic reactions. When wheat is processed with other ingredients (mainly water) the protein in wheat creates gluten. Gluten can also come from barley, rye and malt as well.

- To simplify gluten-free baking, simply mix well 24 ounces of brown rice flour with 16 ounces of cornstarch as a substitute for any flour.

- When substituting for a cup of all-purpose flour in a recipe, remember this mixture weighs less than a regular cup. So here is your substitution ratio:

- 1 cup all-purpose flour = 1 1/4 cup of the rice flour/cornstarch mixture

- 1/4 cup all-purpose flour = 1/4 cup plus 1 tablespoon of the rice flour/cornstarch mixture

Basic Flour Conversions...

Here are a few helpful conversions, when you misplace that measuring cup:

- 3 teaspoons = 1 tablespoon

- 4 tablespoons = 1/4 cup

- 5 tablespoons + 1 teaspoon = 1/3 cup

- 2 cups = 1 pint

- 2 pints = 1 quart

- 4 quarts = 1 gallon

Baking Techniques...

- When it comes to baking, technique is everything.

- Be sure to take your time and read the recipe. Don't underestimate this step.

- Also, mise en place plays a huge role in baking. This is so important in cooking and baking that as a chef I want to get it tattooed on my arm for everyone to see as I cook. Make sure that you have everything you need! I can't say this enough.

- Mise en place, in baking or cooking anything, is all about having all of your ingredients prepped, softened, melted, sifted, and measured before you begin baking. This is the perfect time to ensure that your baking will come out the best that can be. This helps to ensure that you aren't missing a step.

- You don't want to miss a step and find out your buttermilk biscuits taste like bricks because you missed an ingredient like buttermilk and you missed a step like sifting the flour.

- If a recipe says to let a batter rest, then, let the batter rest! Many baking failures come from poor technique, not from poor recipes.

- Unless otherwise stated, use room temperature ingredients.

- If something is meant to be used cold, then, a recipe should state that, otherwise make sure your eggs, butter, sour cream, etc. are room temperature.

- Do not over-mix your batters.

- Use salt (but not table salt)! It is very important to balance the flavors of sweet baked goods. Kosher salt, or medium coarse sea salt, is best.

- Baking powder and baking soda are different ingredients. Pay attention! They serve the same purpose but do not react the same way in baked goods.

- Do you know the difference between baking soda and baking powder? Baking soda needs an acidic ingredient like lemon juice to activate it. Baking powder is baking soda with this acid already built in. They are not interchangeable.

- If you can't remember all of that when it comes to baking, remember this... Baking soda makes things spread like cookies. Baking powder makes things rise like cakes.

- Make baking your own! Just because baking is all about technique doesn't mean you can't get creative with the ingredients that only affect the flavor.

- Change up the extracts, spices, and other add-ins that only affect the flavor of the baked good to make it your own.

- The quality of ingredients is very important.

- All ovens are different. Do not rely on the time in the recipe to work for your oven. Set your timer for several minutes before it says it will be done just to make sure you don't overcook anything.

- Flour should always be measured after being sifted, or, at least, fluffed up.

- You can substitute apple sauce for oil in some recipes.

- When measuring flour, lightly spoon it into the measuring cup and level it off.

- Weighing flour is actually the best way to measure it. So if the recipe gives a weight for the flour go with that if possible.

- Lastly, baking should be fun, not stressful. If it stresses you out, you are doing something wrong.

Meal Quick Fixes 101...

Everyone has experienced that dreadful moment in the kitchen when a recipe failed and dinner guests have arrived.

Perhaps it was a failed timer, distraction or a missing or improperly measured ingredient is to blame. These handy tips can save the day...

- **Acidic foods...** Sometimes a tomato-based sauce will become too acidic. Add baking soda, one teaspoon at a time, to the sauce. Use sugar as a sweet alternative.

- **Burnt food on pots and pans...** Allow pan or pot to cool on its own. Remove as much of the food as possible. Fill with hot water and add a cap full of liquid fabric softener to the pot. Let it stand for a few hours and you will have an easier time removing the burnt food. Wash the pot or pan as you usually would.

- **Chocolate seizes...** Chocolate can seize (turn coarse and grainy) when it comes into contact with water. Place seized chocolate in a metal bowl over a large sauce pan with an inch of simmering water in the pan. Over medium heat slowly whisk in heavy cream. Use one fourth of a cup of cream for every 4 ounces of chocolate. The chocolate will melt and become smooth.

- **Forgot to thaw a whipped topping...** Thaw in the microwave for 1 minute on the defrost setting. Stir to blend well. Do not over thaw.

- **Hands smell like garlic or onion...** Rinse hands under cold water while rubbing them with a large stainless steel spoon.

- **Hard brown sugar...** Place in a brown paper bag and microwave for a few seconds, or place hard chunks in a food processor.

- **Jell-O too hard...** Heat on a low microwave power for a very short time.

- **Lumpy gravy or sauce...** Use a blender, food processor or simply strain.

- **No tomato juice...** Use ½ cup ketchup and ½ cup of water.

- **Out of honey...** Use 1 1/14 cup of sugar dissolved in 1 cup of water.

- **Overcooked sweet potatoes and carrots...** Soften sweet potatoes or carrots make a wonderful soufflé with the addition of eggs and sugar. Overcooked sweet potatoes can also make a great pie filling.

- **Sandwich bread is stale...** Toast or microwave the bread briefly. Otherwise, turn it into bread crumbs. Heat and light will hasten bread's demise so consider using a bread box. Or freeze extra loaves of bread and when you need it, let it thaw naturally. It will taste just like you just bought it.

- **Soups, sauces and gravies too thin...** Add 1 tablespoon flour to hot soup, sauce and gravy, Whisk well to avoid lumps while the mixture is boiling. Repeat steps, if necessary.

- **Sticky rice...** Rinse rice with warm water.

- **Stew or soup too greasy...** Refrigerate and remove grease once it congeals. Another trick is to lay a cold lettuce leaf over the hot stew for about ten seconds, and then, remove it. Repeat it as necessary.

- **Too salty...** Add a little sugar and vinegar. For soups and sauces, add a raw peeled potato.

- **Too sweet...** Add vinegar or lemon juice.

- **Under-cooked cakes or cookies...** Serve with vanilla ice cream. You can also layer pieces of cake or cookies with whipped cream and fresh fruit to form a dessert parfait. Crumbled cookies also make an excellent ice cream or cream pie topping.

On Sale Now...

"Simple, Healthy& Delicious..."

The Hungry Chick Dieting Solution Cookbook!

Chef Jai Scovers shares her favorite most satisfying, delicious recipes, quick meal ideas and helpful cooking tips in her full color, new cookbook... "Simple, Healthy & Delicious"

That will not only help you maintain your healthy weight loss, but provide real meals that your entire family can still enjoy at any time!

Buy Your Copy Right Now!

Here Is A Sneak Peak...

Ham & Herbed Cheese

Yield: 10 servings

Special Diet Information:

How about this light delicious appetizer with just 3 ingredients, ham, herb cheese and cucumber

Ingredients:

- 1 cucumber
- 1 slice of ham
- 10 teaspoons herb cheese (like 'Boursin')
- 1 teaspoon dried parsley (optional)

Directions:

- With a potato peeler, remove randomly some strips of skin of the cucumber to reduce some of the bitterness.
- Slice cucumber into semi-thick slices.
- Slice ham in little strips.
- Place little piles on top of each cucumber slice
- Place now half a teaspoon of herb cheese on top of each little pile of ham.
- Top off with some dried parsley, if desired.
- Enjoy!

Bow Tie Salad

Yield: 8 servings

Special Diet Information:

It takes just just minutes to toss together, but, this salad boasts a whole lot of flavor!

Ingredients:

- 1 pound bow tie pasta
- 2 cucumbers, diced
- 2 grape tomatoes, chopped
- 1 small red onion, diced
- 1 16 oz. bottle creamy Italian dressing
- 1 packet of Italian herb mix
- 1 pound cooked chicken, chopped or salad shrimp

Directions:

- Cook the bow tie pasta according to the package directions.
- Rinse in cold water.
- Add dressing and mix well.
- Add all other ingredients and mix well.
- Season with Italian herb mix
- Refrigerate.
- Enjoy!

Picante Beef Steaks with Sautéed Onions

Yield: 4 servings

Special Diet Information:

The bold flavor will make this steak dish a favorite!

Ingredients:

- 1 tablespoon olive oil
- 1 boneless beef sirloin steak, 3/4-in. thick (about 1-lb.), cut into 4 pieces
- 1 medium onion, cut in half and thinly sliced
- 1 cup Picante Sauce

Directions:

- Heat half the oil in a 12-inch skillet over medium-high heat.
- Add the beef and cook until browned on both sides.
- Remove the beef from the skillet and pour off any fat.
- Reduce the heat to medium.
- Heat the remaining oil in the skillet.
- Add the onion and cook until tender.
- Stir the Picante sauce in the skillet.
- Return the beef to the skillet.
- Cook the beef until desired doneness.
- Enjoy!

About Chef Jai Scovers...

Chef Jai Scovers (pronounced Jay Scoh-Vers) is a trained gourmet chef and a graduate of the world famous Restaurant School at Walnut Hill College in Philadelphia, Pennsylvania, where she was trained in every aspect of the food industry, including food selection, recipe development and menu planning and the nutritional value of food.

Chef Jai has worked to develop her skills in such well-known and recognized dining establishments, as the famed Stephen Starr restaurants to Harrah's Showboat Hotel and Casino in Atlantic City, New Jersey.

She currently holds her nationally recognized ServSafe certification. This certification demonstrates her ability and commitment to food safety, in the areas of food storage, preparation, cleaning, sanitizing and cooking.

Chef Jai Scovers is an advocate in the fight against preventing food borne illnesses and raising awareness about healthy eating. Awareness brings about change. She is also a supporter of several women based charities and fighting childhood hunger.

Proceeds from the sale of every copy of this book sold will go to support several charitable efforts, including, but not limited to, the race to find a cure for breast cancer, ending domestic violence and supporting local food banks to feed hungry families.

Thank you for your support. Your support will allow these charities to help so many more people.

On Sale Now...

"The Hungry Chick Dieting Solution"

Whoever Said That You Should Have To Starve Yourself Just To Lose A Few Unwanted Pounds?

Only in "The Hungry Chick Dieting Solution," the new #1 weight loss guide to help you lose up to 50 of your most suborn, unwanted pounds, will you discover why every diet that you have ever tried, until now, has failed, what your ideal or goal weight should be and how to find out how much water you should really be drinking to stay healthy. It is not the eight glasses of water a day that you have been lied to about!

Buy Your Copy Right Now!

9 780979 930256